TREASURES ON EARTH
Museums, Collections and Paradoxes

KEITH S. THOMSON

faber and faber

First published in 2002
by Faber and Faber Limited
3 Queen Square London WC1N 3AU

Typeset by Faber and Faber in Utopia
Printed in England by Clays Ltd, St Ives plc

© Keith S. Thomson, 2002

The right of Keith S. Thomson to be identified as author
of this work has been asserted in accordance with Section 77
of the Copyright, Designs and Patents Act 1988

A CIP record for this book
is available from the British Library

ISBN 0–571–21295–6

2 4 6 8 10 9 7 5 3 1

TREASURES ON EARTH

As a museum director and scientist in both Britain and the United States, Professor Thomson has a unique perspective on the dilemmas facing our museums. At Yale University he was Professor of Biology, Director of the Peabody Museum of Natural History, and Dean of the Graduate School of Arts and Sciences. After a period as President of the Academy of Natural Sciences of Philadelphia and Distinguished Scientist-in-Residence at the New School for Social Research, he is currently Director of the Oxford University Museum.

Contents

Preface

In writing an essay like this, a set of opinions that has developed over a number of years, the potential list of people to be acknowledged is enormous. Almost everyone I know in the museum world has indirectly helped me write this – and many would be horrified to hear it. I must, however, single out a few people for their special roles.

At the British Museum (Natural History) and at Harvard University, Humphrey Greenwood, Colin Patterson and Alfred Sherwood Romer were my mentors, guides and models as I entered the museum profession. At Yale University, Presidents Kingman Brewster Jr and A. Bartlett (Bart) Giamatti particularly encouraged me and valued the work of the Peabody Museum of Natural History. Without my students there, I would have accomplished very little. At the Academy of Natural Sciences of Philadelphia, Marvin Heaps and John Schmidt, in successive terms as chairmen of the Board of Trustees, conjured up an all-too-brief period when creativity and imagination were encouraged and rewarded. At the New School for Social Research in New York, Jonathan Fanton and Bea Banu provided another wonderful environment in which to teach and write. My colleagues at Oxford, particularly Jim Kennedy, Steve Simpson, Tom Kemp, Wendy Shepherd, Janet Stott, Michael O'Hanlon, Christopher Brown and Jim Bennett, have patiently reintroduced me to life in an English museum, while Lord Evans (Matthew), Stuart Davies, Kate Arnold-Forster and Sophia Mirchandani renewed my acquaintance with British governmental support of museums. Eleanor Sepanski provided a key quotation. Many friends, notably including Robert McCracken Peck, suffered through too many endless dinner table discussions about museums, as have my long-suffering wife and daughters. Linda Thomson Black (no relation), my agent Felicity Bryan, and Lord Evans provided the much-needed encouragement to finish off a project that was long overdue.

Introduction

Hell is paved with good intentions, not with bad ones.
George Bernard Shaw, *Maxims for Revolutionists*, 1903

Museums, at best, are magical places, repositories for the wonders of the world, dynamic participants in our interpretations of the past, and places for launching dreams of the future. They open before us a cornucopia of the materials from millennia of civilization and a billion or so years of earth history. Through museums, we can experience worlds stretching far beyond our immediate lives.

At their worst, museums are perceived as dull, dusty places – institutional attics – where the past is stored but rarely consulted; useful places for society to keep things that must be kept, even though no one uses them.

If you should want to see Guy Fawkes' lantern, Abraham Lincoln's hat, a Holbein portrait of Henry VIII, the gun that killed Kennedy, sunflowers by van Gogh or soup cans by Warhol, the commodes of kings and the leg irons of slaves, fossil dinosaurs and live insects; if you want to learn about peoples native to every part of the world, wars, the Holocaust, the life works of geniuses and eccentrics, the mushroom, the potato, every kind of gun, agricultural implements, the motor car (of course) and train – everything from soup to nuts and the proverbial kitchen sink – the relevant objects have been collected and cared for in museums, libraries, research foundations, archives and historic sites. For every kind of object from old radios to Old Masters that someone has thought worth collecting, somewhere there is an institution dedicated to it.

Good or bad, museums are always in the news, especially for

their acquisitions. Whether it be paintings and sculptures worth a king's ransom, Roman coins, classic motor cars, dinosaurs or the humbler objects of everyday life, the flow of unique objects into our museums is always in the news. Museums are visited by thousands of millions of people every year. In Britain alone there are some 80 million museum visits each year. Any one of the great international museums in London and New York counts its visitors in the several millions; our local historical museum may have more modest attendances, but no less enthusiastic audiences.

There is a great number of museums, perhaps as many as 15,000[1] institutions in the United States and more than 2500 in Great Britain alone (the worldwide number may be unknowable). And the numbers are growing. There was a period in the 1980s to early 1990s when a new museum was being founded more or less every day.[2] New museums still arise every week or so, together with their cousins the science, nature and heritage 'centres' (which differ from museums principally in the emphasis they place on the use of their collections).

We love museums, and we value the objects in them. How can it be, then, that for every newspaper headline announcing some new triumph in the world of museums, there is another bewailing the dire straits in which museums find themselves: decaying, overcrowded buildings; shortage of specialist staff; declining visitor numbers and – at the base of it all – insufficient funds? As we live in a highly materialist world, our enthusiasm for the physical objects of culture and nature is hardly surprising. All should be well in the gifted world of museums. Whether all *is* well in this wonderful world, however, is a different question. Even a cursory look at museums in Britain and America reveals a story of dwindling resources, increasing responsibilities and heightened competition. Some museums are failing, others have already failed. Of 348 British local authority-funded museums sampled in 1963, 39 had closed by 1999, but another 117 had been founded.[3] We are still opening new museums while existing museums are still in trouble.

An examination of the plight of museums, especially the smaller museums outside the major cities, shows that all the wealth of our magnificent collections comes at an enormous cost in terms of time and money. It also carries with it some disturbing growth trends and depends on a largely unstated set of objectives. Museums and related institutions may be on one of those roads that (in the familiar form of the quote given above) are paved with good intentions and pot-holed with unintended consequences. This paradox, between the richness of our collected heritage and the biblical loaves and fishes with which we try to support them, is the subject of this book.

If museums truly hold and interpret our past and present, and can play a major role in shaping our cultural futures, what has gone wrong in paradise? Why is society so supportive of our cultural heritage in principle and apparently so careless in practice? Do we have the wrong kinds of museums? Too many museums? Are we simply backward in recognizing and funding the treasures we already have? Have museums lost track of what the public wants? Have they failed to keep up with changing society and community needs? If things are bad now, what of the future? What will museums collect and how will they interpret their collections in the future? Should there, even, *be* more museums?

Many scholarly books have been written by museum professionals on every aspect of what is, incontrovertibly, a modern growth industry, although I do not imagine that these works find a wide readership among typical museum-goers.[4] This is not a book to be added to that august list. As a scholar, my whole career has depended upon museum collections and I have done my best to add to various collections in my own field. I have spent all my professional life working in and around museums as a research user, a teacher, a curator, a director and simply an avid visitor; but I am a scientist and would not presume to call myself a theorist or philosopher of the subject. Rather, I have found it instructive to step slightly outside the charmed inner circle and to examine museums and related institutions from a different viewpoint. My intended audience is the public who use museums and support them both directly through their gifts and indirectly through taxation. Public visitors to museums outnumber the scholarly users by many thousands to one. That public has a right to ask a lot of museums. While the present may seem rosy in many ways, my view of the future is more bleak. In approaching the subject as much as a consumer as a provider, I have found that the answers called for less rather than more in an industry where 'more' has always been the watchword.

This book is intended for readers on both sides of the Atlantic, where collections, museums and related institutions have much in common and some elements that are totally different. Famously, the tax regime in the United States favours donations to cultural institutions in ways that do not apply in Britain, and it sometimes comes as a surprise to Europeans, used to governmental ownership of museums, that almost all the best American museums (apart from the nationals in Washington DC) are privately funded trusts. Many of the examples I cite are taken from the USA, partly because I know them and partly to invite British readers to find points of comparison with institutions at home.

Throughout this short book, wherever I use the term 'museum' I am really referring to a huge, sprawling class of institutions that preserve, and create a use for, materials of our cultural heritage. This would include zoos and botanical gardens, but we might exclude those institutions that are not defined in any strict sense by 'collections' of objects held with any sense of perpetuity. Thus science centres may not have permanent collections but only disposable ones. On the other hand, an opera house may have an important collection of archives, photographs and costumes. Libraries and archives obviously fall within my definition, although they tend to fall outside the strictures of my conclusions. Suffice it to say that I use the term 'museum' for all those kinds of institutions whose business includes the holding and use of material cultural collections.

1
Museums and Collections

Lay not up for yourselves treasures upon earth where moth
and rust doth corrupt.
The Gospel according to St Matthew, 6:19

Material 'things' – artistic, natural, historical, technological, frivolous, serious, dead or alive, sublime or trivial – occupy a place of unusual importance in our twenty-first-century lives. Not only do we create and use material objects on a scale never seen before, we also study them intensively and collect them passionately. As a result, the institutions that hold these objects for the public play an ever-growing role in the collection, preservation, study, interpretation and enjoyment of all this richness of nature and talent.

The collections held in our public institutions form a treasure beyond the dreams of avarice, comprising perhaps more than a billion paintings, drawings, prints and sculptures, thousands of houses and estates, countless antiquities, ethnographic and archaeological specimens, far more than a billion natural history specimens alone. Emperors and barbarians of previous ages would have killed for such treasures – indeed emperors and barbarians *did* loot and kill, cheat and steal for many of them, often in the name of civilization and often quite recently. These objects form an almost unimaginable wealth of craftsmanship, inspiration and genius. While nature in all its wonder created some, honest toil created the rest; some emerged from the depths of maddened loneliness, others in the giddy height of fashion. All these treasures of nature and artifice (plus a great deal of the lesser debris of human affairs) are the material manifestation of something intangible and precious: our cultural heritage. They are us.

1

But these cultural materials represent more than the heritage of the countries that currently house them, for these objects have often travelled far and wide. Indeed, because of the vagaries of history and the rise and fall of empires, peoples of other countries must often come to Western Europe or the United States to see and study portions of their own birthrights. For example, American and British collections arguably contain as fine assemblages of French Impressionist paintings as can be found in France, more dinosaurs from Mongolia than exist in Asia (except in the ground, of course), and the most complete representations of the natural history (much of it now extinct) of regions of the world from Spitzbergen to Australia.

While one measure of the 'wealth of nations' is in terms of millions of bushels of corn, numbers of fighter planes and oil tankers, reserves of gold and natural gas, or the production of better television sets, it is actually judged not simply by things – not even by the accumulation of the objects of our high cultures – but by moral and noble ideas and our commitments to them. In an important sense, our material creations offer far more than just a documentation of what is and was. They constitute an ongoing test of ideas and aesthetic values. Material objects as elevated as a sculpture by a master or as commonplace as a household implement burnished by years of unrewarded toil express what we are and what we wish to be: a celebration as well as a testimony.

How does a society own these materials? The rich own some of them outright; most of us own them in a peculiarly vicarious way, not so much individually as jointly. Governments (national and local), charitable trusts, and individuals all create or support for this purpose museums and other institutions, almost as secular temples, charging them to create and hold collections and to define their role in our lives. The 'business' of all these objects has created an immense proliferation of institutions to which we accord a strange status, half public and half private: museums, libraries, research foundations, botanical gardens, zoos, historic houses, ships . . . the list is endless. Such institutions are private if they are not (or at least not wholly) owned or supported by any arm of the public acting directly through a governmental agency. But all are public institutions in the sense that they are said to hold collections in public trust and may be (but not wholly) supported by the public as individuals and by taxes. Who truly owns them is, therefore, paradoxical.

The purposes of museums are as diverse as their collections. Not only do they collect and display, they teach, conduct research, entertain and publish. You can hire a hall in a museum for a wedding or a child's birthday party. Businesses use museum auditoria for annual meetings or to launch new products. Museums can be deadly earnest (not always intentionally) or playful. All this is done on a scale ranging from the gigantic to a one-room cabin. Do we know why we create and support these expensive institutions? Why do we want to store *all* those expensive objects so expensively in museums? Why do we collect and save objects so avidly?

Fundamentally, museums exist for far more purposes than simply to have and to hold cultural objects. At their core, the arts and sciences (writ large) are not universally accessible – that is to say, they require interpretation and explication. Museums are major players in that process – eager intermediaries indeed, using all the skills of display, interpretation, informal and formal teaching, marketing, and just plain inspiration that they can muster. Museums act as brokers and suppliers in the world of information. Contrary to uninformed opinion, the objects held in our collections are not simply a series of static, fixed points in our culture, like grave-markers in our history. Instead, they are constantly open to interpretation and re-interpretation. It is in this constant shifting of interpretations and contexts that museums play their role in shaping our understanding of the present and future. For example, the story told by a First World War rifle from Mons or Ypres is not just a documentary reminder of long-ago horror and sacrifice, but a cautionary tale for the future. Today we see that rifle quite differently from the way people saw it fifty years ago, or from the ways it will be seen in the future. We would think about it differently again if we did not have the physical object in front of us. This does not mean that all value and meaning is relative, but neither is it all fixed in stone. Through their objects and the interpretation of objects in a nested set of cultural contexts, museums become the active link between cultural objects and the public, especially as essential partners with the print and broadcasting media. And while museums often seem to reinforce conventional views of society they also, especially through the arts, challenge the status quo and promote change.

Museums are unique in that they accomplish their work by the agency of the authentic objects of the arts and sciences. In a word, museums have and use the *real thing* – not pictures of things, not representations of things, not virtual but actual. And because of the immediacy and authenticity of their working materials – because of their role as a living link with the past, and because of our fascination with the beautiful, the rare, and (it has to be admitted) the fabulously valuable – museums occupy a strange and complex place in contemporary culture. A museum is at once sacred cow, symbol of elitism and exclusivity, creator of popular taste, pride of the city or village, financial black hole, grateful recipient of private charity and public tax subsidy, educational resource, archive of scholarly information, place of entertainment, hobby of the mighty and passion of volunteers. Even the poorest museum to some degree plays a special role in the expression of our culture. At their best museums are wondrous places that bring us face to face with our own greatness and that of our forebears. They may also, of course, show us at our worst, because objects can be used to reveal, and sometimes explain, our weaknesses as well as our strengths.

2

Museums at First Hand

'Myself when young did eagerly frequent Doctor and Saint, and heard
great argument . . .'
Edward FitzGerald, *The Rubáiyát of Omar Khayyám*, 1859

Because some of my criticisms of the 'museum business' are harsh, I feel it is necessary to present my credentials and perhaps also to convey something of the romance and lure of museums for me.

I have spent all my professional life in museums and among museum people. My first paid employment was in the British Museum (Natural History) in London (or, as it is now called, The Natural History Museum) in the summer between my second and third years as an undergraduate at the University of Birmingham. I never fully left. As a graduate student at Harvard University, my office was in the Museum of Comparative Zoology – the Agassiz Museum – occupying with its four sister museums a prime spot at the end of Oxford Street away from the tacky crowds of Harvard Square but handy for all the libraries.

As a NATO post-doctoral research fellow, I was based back in London at University College, but spent much time in my old haunts at the BM(NH). As a faculty member at Yale University I was both professor of biology and a curator at the Peabody Museum of Natural History, an institution I later directed. Having two roles there merely doubled the workload, a common enough situation in most museums. In Philadelphia I was President and CEO of the Academy of Natural Sciences for nine years. Now I direct one of Europe's great natural history museums, at the University of Oxford.

Even the public spaces of museums have a special feel, a special smell, a different light and even their own sounds. But when you venture behind those closed doors at the ends of the galleries, they are very different again. Together, halls and offices, library and workshop, museum shop to the furthest collection rooms, all museums have a special feel. Additionally, natural history museums have some added behind-the-scenes odours – the hard scent of insect repellents like paradichlorbenzene (mothballs, now no longer used), the acrid bite of formaldehyde, the sickly sweetness of alcohol.

And then there are the seasonal rhythms. In a public institution you quickly come to tell the seasons by the noise in the exhibition halls, which peaks in the spring as teachers tend to bring their classes on more field trips. For some reason, children always shout louder on rainy days. The state of the internal economy can be monitored on the basis of the number of school buses parked outside at mid-morning, and the glossier tour buses on summer afternoons. In the research spaces, activity grows in the summer months with the influx of visiting academics while, in northern museums, the resident scholars tend to travel in mid-winter. By amazing good fortune their work seems to take them to places warm and exotic (as a price for this, they do it all on a shoestring budget). The whole staff rallies around to help with the latest travelling exhibit, a fund-raising event, or to see some prize object newly arrived from foreign parts. Museum people are unusually interested in the history of their own institutions and just as exciting as the latest acquisition is the discovery in the archives of an old letter from Charles Demuth or Charles Darwin, or a lost photograph of Rodin. Museums have a mystique, a special power that comes from the association with all those great 'things' and, truth be told, museums are even more fun for their inmates than they are for their visitors.

When I was a little boy, my family lived in the English Midlands.

Visits to museums meant London, and that meant a wait until the war was over (the Second World War, that is). After the war, railway journeys on trains powered by roaring steam locomotives with romantic names like 'The Duchess of Atholl' took us south to the capital. I remember long, uncomfortable journeys on trains crowded with standing people, often soldiers in rough khaki uniforms, cinders pouring through the open windows of ancient carriages decorated with advertisements for impossible pre-war holidays on the deep south coasts of Devon and Cornwall. (I hope a set of those posters has been preserved in a museum somewhere!)

My father and mother had taken a curious set against two of the London museums that later became important to me. My father avoided the main Bloomsbury branch of the British Museum on the grounds that it was all too academic for our tender minds (although I suspect that he wanted to shield my sister and me from depictions of naked people). My mother disliked stuffed birds and animals – 'poor little things' – so we *never* went to the Natural History branch in South Kensington. But all was not lost. My father, although a Baptist minister, was an inventor manqué who at the age of fourteen had published an account of a way of linking a variable condenser to the old-fashioned crystal-set wireless. So for us there was no choice, we headed for the Science Museum, just around the corner from the as yet unseen wonders of natural history.

At the Science Museum we gazed in awe at Stephenson's Rocket and regularly returned to a magnificent gallery full of model steam locomotives powered at the press of a button by compressed air (which, as is always the case in museums, often didn't work!). We looked with respect and a great deal of puzzlement at Newcomen's engine, the scientific and social-historical significance of which was not well explained, especially to a small boy who wanted it to do something other than move a beam and piston ponderously up and down. Those models and real machines were, in a special sense, mine. I took away no specific message from each visit. It was a little like being in church – hushed voices, solemn movements. But it was immensely powerful and exciting. I was part of a wider and – this is the crucial word – deeper reality, even though it was years before I made the intellectual connections among the concepts of heat, energy and work. The impressive feature of these machines was simply the translation of movement – small to large, lines into circles. Mechanics, that is, not thermodynamics; facts, not ideas.

It was not until I was aged perhaps thirteen that a school trip finally revealed to me the glories of naked ladies in marble and in pigmented oil on canvas. It was a visit to Chatsworth House, Derbyshire. Nowadays thousands of people pour through the house and gardens and the fountains are reckoned a special treat. In those austere post-war days, visitors were few and the fountains didn't work. But the paintings and sculpture did. When I graduated from my distinguished if unimaginative school, I was awarded the sixth form science prize, a book of my choosing. To considerable consternation, I asked for the book to be E. M. Gombrich's classic, *The Story of Art*. To be fair, it may be a little harsh to call the school unimaginative. After all, I and others left with a strong taste for both the art museum and the concert hall. None the less, I was probably very fortunate to go to university in Birmingham, with its superb city art gallery and the Barber Institute of Fine Arts. On fine days and rainy (there being no shortage of the latter) I discovered not just the pleasures of the individual objects on display but that sense of half-possession we call the museum experience.

Soon I discovered the even more powerful lure of a museum, in its private nether regions where the collections are stored and worked on. In early July 1959 I presented myself as a newly appointed Vacation Student at the door of the Keeper of Zoology, British Museum (Natural History), an institution through whose doors I had walked only once before. And so I discovered the true romance of a museum.

How else but romantically could one feel about an institution that in 1959 was directed by the portly Sir Gavin de Beer (Sir Cumference, as he was privately known), zoologist, embryologist and lately historian of science. In those days, each morning at exactly 9.55 a.m. a uniformed porter at the sidewalk gate would peer out towards the corner of Exhibition Road. At 9.56, an elderly Rolls-Royce, the sort with rows of shining silver rivets down the centre of the bonnet, made the turn and progressed in stately fashion down Cromwell Road. The porter drew back the large iron gates – otherwise closed against the *hoi polloi*. The car was parked (whether by a chauffeur or not, I cannot remember) and the great man proceeded up the steps in as grand a manner as possible for someone with short legs. There the number two porter said 'Good morning, sir' and held open the door. The head porter gave Sir Gavin a large bunch of old-fashioned brass keys and, by unique privilege, opened the gate to the small lift that led to the Director's office. At 5 p.m. the ritual was repeated in reverse. What happened in between, nobody seemed to know, but sherry was mentioned.

I was not destined to meet that great man (at least not then). Instead I was dispatched with considerably less ceremony through endless empty halls with their guards waiting for the daily onslaught of children, to a small door in the wall and, beyond, to the office of the Keeper of Zoology, Dr Frazer. Frazer was a jolly Scot on the inside and a proper member of the Establishment on the outside. His office was exactly as I had imagined it – glass-fronted, dark mahogany bookcases, a fine Turkish rug, piles of leather-bound books, the smell of wax polish and just a touch of formaldehyde. He in turn (still no sherry) summoned an irreverent young South African ichthyologist, Peter Humphrey (Humph) Greenwood, and after an interesting exchange of ribald jokes between the two, Greenwood led me off to the Spirit Building.

The Spirit Building at the BM(NH) is one of the centres of its museum-ness. It stands at the back of the museum looking into the rear windows of what was then the Geology Museum, separated by a car park with war-time prefabricated huts reputed to contain material from the expedition of HMS *Challenger* (1872–76). Inside are many floors filled (to the gills, so to speak) with thousands upon thousands of fishes preserved in alcohol – the non-potable kind but highly flammable, hence the heavily barred windows. The smell of the Spirit Building is a mixture of the tang of alcohols plus the sweet odour of decay. There is no building in the world with the special smell of the Spirit Building although every spirit collection in every natural history museum has something of its quality.

In the adjacent building were the offices of the experts in fishes, mammals, frogs, snakes and who knew what else. All rather odd characters, with cultivated eccentricities and very shabby clothes. Presiding over all, informally if not formally, was Dr E. Trevawas – 'Auntie Ethelwyn' – without whose sympathetic coaching I would surely have gone home that first day and never returned.

Connecting the Spirit Building to the rest of the baffling complex forming the dusty bowels of the Museum is a low colonnaded walkway, reminiscent of an abandoned subway station. Here Greenwood and I would pace for hours each day, furiously smoking cigarettes and talking (me listening) about science. Or we would explore the nearby storage areas with their mysterious packing cases labelled 'Tibet' or 'Persia', wounded mammals with their stuffing showing, and rocks too large to store anywhere else. Here the smells were a blend of dust, plaster, old dry wood, coffee, mothballs and just a hint of paint. These cavernous cellars had a special timeless feel; nothing seemed to change even though crates came and went, and workmen in those old-fashioned European brown housecoats always looked reasonably busy. It all seemed suspended in time. Occasionally there flitted through it members of a veritable college of scholars, none too famous or busy (though famous and busy they were) to talk with a gangly student.

In those first weeks I certainly embraced the romance of museums but I also learned some of the problems. The high security was a barrier to a true ebb and flow of the inmate scholars. Everywhere there were solid doors only to be opened with huge brass keys – the badge of office of the established curator. People stayed in their own little areas with the result that palaeontologists and entomologists hardly knew each other. Happily this all changed with the influx of energetic new curators like Greenwood and Colin Patterson now, sadly, both deceased.

Humphrey Greenwood was very fond of the old Hall of Fishes, a long room of low, glass-lidded mahogany cabinets filled with mounted fishes of every shape and size, and elaborate demonstrations of internal anatomy and behaviour. Good, solid 1920s stuff, in a style little changed from 1880. Around that time, some young whipper-snappers in the exhibits department decided to tear it all out and put in something 'exciting'. Over Greenwood's dead body, almost. In the end, of course, the hall was gutted and then stayed empty for years while whipper-snappers came and left. No matter how hard anyone tried to develop a 'modern', 'exciting' alternative for synoptic halls like those old ones, they always seemed to lack something. The bolder the experiment, the deeper the failure.

Part of the romance, and the material difficulty, was the building itself. The BM(NH) is a superb piece of richly ornamented, high Victorian architecture, perfectly suited to synoptic exhibits in glowing mahogany cabinets. Indeed the very columns are carved with climbing lizards, plants, snakes and insects. But hopeless for the age of 'Danish modern', Formica and stainless steel. Over the years, the critical injunction to 'never deny the building' was daily neglected. The museum seems never to have recovered from those early innovations. Once its Victorian integrity of style was lost, nothing could bring it back. But possibly only grumpy old-

timers like me look at the architecture; most visitors happily con-
centrate on the displays.

In most bigger museums, the curators either feel that they are
left out of the exhibit planning process or, when they are asked to
take charge of something, grumble about the time involved and
the compromises they must make. I hope my friends will forgive
me when I say also that, as is usual in any academic situation –
museum or university – most people in positions of authority
(directors especially!) are there because of their accomplishment
in something else. Following the Peter Principle, no one except the
curators and technical staffs are professionals in their work. In
such situations, museums call in outside experts to 'jazz up' the
exhibit halls, people who have done wonderful things with trade
shows and television specials, but whose approach to museums is
largely, and literally, iconoclastic.

I observed all of this as a nineteen-year-old and knew, from that
first week, that museums were where I wanted to be – problems,
paradoxes and all.

A lot of the old ways of doing things still persist, or a hankering for
them, and a crucial problem now for all museums concerns the
capacity and will to change. Most museums have assimilated
modern display and design techniques, but have not come to
terms with the growth of their collections. After all, museums are
quintessentially for *stability*. How can you be stable *and* change?
That is every museum's question and every museum's nightmare.

A second problem is conceptual: what should the mission of
museums be? In their heyday, museums opened up worlds that
were otherwise inaccessible. In art museums the great paintings of
the world could be seen in a glory that no one had yet managed to
reproduce on posters and postcards. In natural history museums
one visited the plains of the Serengeti or the Gobi Desert vicari-
ously by means of great glass-fronted dioramas. Synoptic displays

of the birds of Tibet, New Jersey or East Africa gave a completeness (and an accessibility) unattainable in the wild. Moreover, museums were one's main chance, outside of books, to experience anything of the past. Apart from the agency of institutions, contact with the 'real thing' in art, archaeology, science or history was something of a rarity. Except for the rich. Nowadays, package tours to Paris or East Africa are widely available. For those who prefer to stay at home, there is the Louvre website or the CD-ROM of the Barnes Collection. Television presents so much 'educational' programming with art, dinosaurs, and living natural history in full colourful motion that a trip to the museum seems flat in comparison. What was inaccessible has become commonplace, and television and movies have blurred the line between fact and fiction, reality and fantasy. Serious problems therefore face an industry built on the past, with a toe-hold in the present, but confronting an inexorable pressure to embrace the future.

3

Some Favourite Museums

Layer upon layer, past times preserve themselves in the city until
life itself is finally threatened with suffocation; then, in sheer defense,
modern man invents the museum.

Lewis Mumford, *The Culture of Cities*, 1938

Throughout this book, for purposes of building up a picture of
the present state of collections and museums in Britain and the
United States, I shall mention a small number that, for one reason
or other, I find particularly attractive or informative. I will start the
ball rolling and provoke argument by introducing five examples of
quite different museums, each of which has analogues in every
country.

While the national newspapers and magazines naturally tend to
cover the great international museums of the world, their dazzling
blockbuster exhibitions and their high-profile fund-raising events,
we should never lose sight of the fact that the overwhelming
majority of museums and collections, in every country, are small
and local. The first 'museum' I ever visited existed as a series of
display cases of local fossils that stood in our local library (alas,
they are no longer there).

Let us take as the first example a museum that I have visited
recently, the Wakefield Museum in Yorkshire. This is a city museum (City of Wakefield Metropolitan District Council), situated
next to the Town Hall, with displays on two floors. Upstairs is the
history of the area from pre-Roman times to the 1987 miners'
strike. On the ground floor there is an especially nice display of the
natural history objects collected by a local hero, Charles Waterton
(1783–1865), who was famous as an explorer and collector long

before Charles Darwin.[5] Here is something for everyone who lives in Wakefield and for every visitor to the area. Particularly appealing are the familiar objects from the last fifty years. No one can enter here without exclaiming 'my grandmother had one just like that' or 'I had forgotten all about those . . .' No one should leave the museum without feeling more secure and at the same time somewhat challenged, for Wakefield has seen its times of glory and sorrow.

Every town should have a museum like this, and most do, although many are less professional and less ambitious. There is one such smaller museum in Harlowton. It could be in the town next door to Wakefield (Hemsworth, perhaps); in fact, it is five thousand miles to the west.

Harlowton, Montana, is a small town of a few thousand souls in American cattle country. Every Fourth of July it puts on a first-rate rodeo and then subsides into a rural tranquillity. Here is a wonderful little treasure of a small-town museum, set in an old liquor store. On two floors one finds all the accumulated home-town treasures of ordinary people in middle America: election buttons, war mementoes, farm implements, local photographic history, some fossils, and the full-size fibreglass replica of a dinosaur found on a local ranch (the original being back east with the institution that collected it). A part-time curator, loyal volunteers, a certain amount of dust, a great deal of nostalgia – wonderful.

Even this brief description of the Harlowton museum instantly brings to mind a hundred others. These are often the first museums one encounters and they remain our favourites, their immediacy and local connections preventing them from being totally replaced in our affections by their glossy metropolitan big sisters. Of course, the Harlowton museum is exactly the sort of downmarket place full of bric-a-brac that I might otherwise snobbishly decry. But it is a collection well matched to its resources and forms no drain on the community. It is unlikely that success will spoil this museum in the immediate future. Equally, at this scale, it is in little danger of becoming an orphan. Could astute development turn the museum into an archive of central Montana history or western American painting and sculpture, or could the rodeo be enlisted to put the museum on the metaphorical map, bringing in thousands of tourists who might otherwise not detour from their route between Billings and Boseman? A new large building, parking lots and a restaurant? How much would it be worth for the town to invest in that? Better to leave it just as it is, as truly a local museum.

Museums tend to be indoor places. The Kimbell Art Museum in Fort Worth, Texas, has the advantage of a superbly inviting building (by Louis Kahn) that effortlessly draws the light inside with the visitor, filtering the harsh north Texas sun through trees and grass. The collection of paintings and sculpture is of just the right scale for its generous endowment and supportive community. The museum has concentrated on quality first, within a relatively narrow range of areas and the greatest of the great artists, rather than growth (although this policy has been controversial). There are no accumulations of reserve collections for study by scholars, everything is devoted to presenting to the public a cross-section of the very best in art. The core of the collections is the bequest from Mr Kay Kimbell, who

> attached no conditions as to the use or retention of his collection . . . he simply mandated the establishment of a museum to encourage art in Fort Worth and Texas. [The aim of the Kimbell] is not historical completeness but the quality of the individual object as determined by its condition, rarity, importance, suitability and communicative powers, i.e. quality . . . the rationale is that individual work of outstanding merits and importance is more effective as an educational tool than a larger number of representative examples.[6]

Over the years, the collection has been upgraded by improving the quality rather than increasing the number of exhibits. For each greater piece acquired, a lesser one has been let go. The result is an unparalleled primer in western art.

Years ago, someone asked me why I enjoyed being a museum director. I answered, no doubt naively, that it offered 'a grand opportunity to exercise one's taste'. The Kimbell is one of the finest examples of taste carefully exercised. It is the institutional equivalent of the personal collection. But more than that, the museum is a place in which all visitors can feel comfortable, welcome and respected. Obviously it is not the only such museum, but it is a welcome antidote to the monolith/mausoleum style of museum in which one feels the dead, authoritarian hand of the ages rather than the breath of a living art.

I have a specially warm spot in my heart for the National Maritime Museum, in Greenwich, England. Some thirty years ago I spent a highly productive time there, rummaging through the files of old ships' plans until I finally stumbled upon the closest thing that exists to the original draughts of Charles Darwin's ship, HMS *Beagle*.[7] One of the great national collections of any kind, anywhere in the world, the National Maritime Museum occupies a magnificent historical building and cares for a superlative collection that stands at the heart of the British sense of self – every British child's schooldays are replete with nautical references: exploration, Drake and the Armada, colonial expansion, fishing fleets, the National Lifeboat Association, Swallows and Amazons, Nelson.

Britain, as a major seafaring island-nation, naturally enough has a super-abundant legacy of boats and ships of every description, from skin coracles and dories to wherries and dinghies, from humble herring drifters to the great clipper ships and the great and small battleships of history, together with the superlative but almost suffocating documentation that goes with them. The

National Maritime Museum is a treasure trove for the public, from children to senior citizens, and an even greater source of bounty for the scholar of maritime history. In fact, it may already be too great a legacy for our capacity to care for it, and the pressure grows each day to add new vessels to the list of those to be preserved. The museum has simply run out of space in London and has embarked on a major plan of devolving whole collections to regional museums. But this only postpones the inevitable: each year harder decisions will have to be made concerning what to save and what to let go. Given this sceptr'd isle's maritime history, which has all of the mythic status of American views of the 'western frontier', controversial days are ahead for this jewel of a museum.

It may not be fair to include an extinct institution, but with his 'Philadelphia Museum' of 1786, Charles Willson Peale famously invented the idea of the museum as public entertainment instead of an institution of private education and self-improvement or the well-meaning condescension of the aristocracy. Known today primarily for the number and brilliance of his paintings (and the number and brilliance of his artistic family), Peale essentially invented the popular public museum and did well out of it. In natural history he pioneered the diorama, the display of natural objects (suitably preserved) in a life-like setting reconstructing the original environment. A bear presented this way was far more dramatic and exciting than a skin in a glass case. Peale developed the art of showmanship and the importance of public relations in art. In other words, Peale was thoroughly modern. His neighbours (and unwilling competitors) at the Academy of Natural Sciences of Philadelphia viewed with proper disdain all that 'vulgar and ephemeral curiosity which manifests itself in a desire to see what is not commonly held in nature, or art'[8] – and then, like every other museum in the world, copied it. He took his museum to Baltimore, where his family continued the tradition, also founding Peale's New York Museum (1825) at 252 Broadway. Various of the collections were eventually sold to P. T. Barnum, who extended the element of 'show-biz' and provided links from Peale, on the one hand to the present American Museum of Natural History, and on the other, to Disneyland.

Peale's creations had a habit of burning down but if there is one museum I would like to visit, via some kind of time travel, it would be Peale's very first museum – Peale's Philadelphia Museum, founded 1786, moved 1802. I would love to watch visitors experience this amazing new phenomenon which featured, among other wonders, the skeleton of a huge fossil mastodon excavated by the polymath Peale in New York State.[9] How far, I wonder, would one discover we had progressed in two hundred years?

4

Reconstructing Reality

It must be clear that it is our business not to supply reality but to invent
allusions to the conceivable which cannot be presented.
Jean-François Lyotard, *The Postmodern Condition:*
A Report on Knowledge, 1993

'Listen,' she concluded, 'I consider the Museum of Jurassic Technology
to be one of the great artistic treasures of the Western World.' As
with everything to do with the MJT, it was hard to tell whether she was
kidding or not.
Lawrence Wechsler, *Mr Wilson's Cabinet of Wonder,* 1996

To the much-invoked mythical person-in-the-street, museums
are surely about objects: they are places where you go to see 'the
real thing'. Over the last fifty years, museums have changed enor-
mously in the ways they deal with 'the real thing' as they assimilate
the techniques and strategies of the theatre, television and advertising, but the person-in-the-street trusts them to ensure that 'the
real thing' is not overwhelmed by the modes of presentation and
interpretation. We all have to ensure that, to recast Marshall
McLuhan's famous dictum, the object remains the message.

The varied institutions we call museums occupy a curious and
ambivalent intellectual territory. On the one hand they seem to
give access to the materials of our cultures, on the other they create a distance between the public and the objects. Our fondest
notion is that these objects, because they are housed in these curious quasi-public institutions, have somehow been made 'ours',
even though in fact they belong to the Duke of This-or-That, or the
Museum of Art in Somewhere City. We therefore share in the ownership of magnificent and beautiful things. Our city or village is the

greater because we have a major art museum, an historic house or treasured local collection. Thereby we share in ownership of wonderful things like Cézanne's *Bathers* or a classic 1930s delivery van. Furthermore, we can visit 'our' painting or object whenever we want (as long as it is on display, of course; if it is in storage the situation may be trickier).

In the late 1970s an authority on children's television came to me and suggested making a film of the Peabody Museum at Yale University. The idea, she explained proudly, was that the film could be taken and shown at schools 'so that they wouldn't have to come in to the museum at all'. She was unhappy with my rather abrupt response. If museums are not a place for the public to see the real thing, what was the point? Today, in the age of the World Wide Web and CD-ROMs, I can call up on my computer screen images of the world's great collections but they still do not substitute for the real thing.

It is a central concept of museums that cultural objects constitute a 'reality'. All we have to do is put them on view somewhere and we will partake of that reality. But what, philosophers will ask, is 'real'? Luckily, museum visitors largely enter unencumbered by the kind of postmodernist doubts about the nature of reality summarized in the statement by Lyotard given above. Whether scholar or tyro, they come principally to see 'the real stuff'. A photograph of the Mona Lisa will not do. In fact, to have seen a hundred reproductions of the Mona Lisa will only whet our appetite one day to go to Paris and see the real thing. In addition, the museum experience carries its own ethos – a value-added experience – by making the visitor feel empowered or, in all too many cases, humbled.

While reality appears to reign triumphant in most museums, it is often curiously denied (apparently without harm) in the natural history museum. Those birds and mammals are only skins mounted on a framework of wire, foam and plaster. When it comes to fossils, *Tyrannosaurus rex*, the *sine qua non* of dinosaurs, exists only in the form of a dozen or so incomplete skeletons (plus some isolated bits and pieces) worldwide. The vast majority of the *T. rex* skeletons oohed and aahed over by generations of schoolchildren are actually duplicate casts in plaster or fibreglass of only two or three specimens, and none of these is complete. Even when a museum has real fossil skeletons in the basement, they are too heavy (being made of stone) to mount in life-like poses, so fibreglass is perhaps essential if all that intrusive supporting ironwork is to be avoided. Of course, casts and copies were previously common in art museums, and it is sometimes confusing to the public that bronze sculptures exist in many copies – for example, all those Degas dancing girls, or bits of Rodin.

We come to see the 'real' paintings, the mummies, the Indian head-dresses, the implements, the dinosaurs. When we look closer at any museum, however, how real is real? Arguably, when all those cultural objects are taken from their original or acquired contexts and placed in institutions, all the institution can do is essentially to establish a series of *reconstructions* of reality. Museums tell a particular story, promote an idea or a value, evoke a particular experience or life, bring back a time or place long gone or create one of the conceivable future by using parts of, or representations of, a real world. When someone like Kenneth Clark or Robert Hughes makes a television series about art or material culture, the reconstruction is more evident, but the same principle applies in the museum, and 'reconstructions of reality' will serve as a shorthand for the whole process.

Even when we view something as apparently straightforward as a painting on the wall of a museum, we are forced to recognize elements of 'reconstruction' and 'story-telling' in its display. When we hang a painting by Monet or Jackson Pollock in a museum, we have taken it from a whole range of realities (the artist's studio, the artist's mind, the artist's environment, friends, influences) and placed it in another set, equally real but for which it may not have been intended. Some modern painters may paint with the notion that the work will only be hung in the isolated off-white spaces of a museum or gallery but most, especially in the past, expected their work to hang with other pictures in libraries, offices or living rooms. A Matisse hanging on a beautifully painted bare wall in London or Paris, nicely lit, with hundreds of visitors shuffling past, is only a new version of the reality that once was the painting forming under the brush of the painter, and then hanging in a house with other pictures, children running around, cigar smoke wafting up from a hundred dinner table conversations. The quiet, almost reverential place in which we now view the picture is sterile in comparison and wholly artificial. A modern trend is to place particularly important paintings in rooms of their own, further increasing this sense of unreality, turning the object into an icon, distancing us from it – all in the name of access.

When the astonishing Barnes Collection of French Impressionist paintings went on international tour, it was beautifully exhibited (in Paris, for example) in the standard museum way – each picture isolated in its own off-white space. Like many others familiar with the original, seemingly appallingly cluttered, Barnes settings in their permanent Pennsylvania home (see page 44), I thought the pictures looked entirely different, yet actually diminished.[10] The Barnes works, therefore, had some original reality or realities, acquired a new reconstructed reality at Barnes' hands, and then found a different one again on tour. The Barnes Collection is, if not a reconstruction, a construction, for, paradoxical as it may seem, a painting is perhaps a bit like the pearl that gains lustre from being worn against the warm skin of a human being: not the fate which the oyster intended for it, but an alternative, and perhaps enhancing, one.

The word 'reality' itself must be qualified because, reconstruct as hard as we may, we are working in the dark. As a scientist, dealing with manipulations of a supposedly concrete material world, I know that reality is a will of the wisp. We all often deal with illusions, often with delusions. Museums are nice places to visit (and even more comfortable in which to work) because they appear to push off to a distance any awkward questions about the nature of reality. Reality is assumed – after all, one has the object in one's hand (almost). It is at these points that I am glad I am a zoologist.

The phrase 'reconstruction of reality' applies to all displays of objects in institutions, not just to dioramas of mounted lions or the skeletons of dinosaurs. Stonehenge exists neither as originally built nor as time had left it (some of the stones have been hoisted back into their original places). Mount Vernon and Monticello are reconstructions too, if only because Washington and Jefferson, their slaves, the smells and sounds of the eighteenth century – to say nothing of their libraries – are missing and we, as visitors, are there. So is Chatsworth, even though the Devonshires still live there.

Some examples of the unreality of museum objects and settings are especially obvious. All of us have visited museums where great old vehicles of the past stand, perfectly restored, not a drop of oil underneath (possibly because there is little inside), never to run again. Sometimes I look at such cars and think (possibly romantically, but my wife and I own a 1947 Chevrolet) it would be better to run the things, run them until their bearings wear out and their chassis buckle. Without the smell of hot oil, the throaty sound of the exhaust, the uncomfortable bounce of those terrible suspensions and the magical combination of the odours of petrol and leather they become like the Mona Lisa behind her heavy security barrier at the Louvre. They might as well be plastic replicas, so far do these superbly polished machines differ from the reality of the highway. Certainly the public can see them. But what we see is only a caricature of the real thing.

In a glass case at a well-known museum in the American Mid-

West,[11] I once saw a set of neglected violins by Guarneri displayed, somewhat ironically, close to some early twentieth-century kitchen objects. Obviously unused for years, they looked dead; they were dead. Worse than highly restored automobiles, they were like those drab, lethargic lions one sees in city zoos, stretched out on concrete 'rocks' under wilting chestnut trees. What was the point of collecting those instruments? If they are not to be played, they should be hidden away so as not to reproach us any more. (This *is* romantic and I fully understand the dilemmas concerning the playing of historic instruments – the balance between damage due to use and damage due to non-use.)

All this may well explain the popularity of working steam trains even though the average journey is only a few miles. What matters is not being transported from A to B and back again, but the sights, smells and especially the sounds of a steam locomotive in action. And how bitterly disappointed we unsophisticates are to arrive on a day when the cars are only to be pulled by a diesel locomotive, no matter how ancient and historically important.

All museums are based on some kind of collection, and usually the objects concerned are tangible and permanent. It is this distinction that makes the definition of zoos and arboreta as museums somewhat problematical, their collections being living and ephemeral. None the less, the animals and plants are real and certainly become part of a reconstructed reality. Even that dusty old lion sitting under a tree in a city zoo represents a kind of reality, however far from the Serengeti plains that concrete and those chestnut trees may be.

The reconstruction of reality can take many forms: the literal reconstruction of a Civil War fort, period tea parties in an historical mansion or exhibitions such as those showing the intellectual links between Rodin and Michelangelo[12] or surprising parallels between the works of Bonnard and Rothko.[13] The most literal reconstructions that museums create involve explicit story-telling.

A group of objects is arranged to make a narrative. We see this implicit in all exhibitions and it is a prominent feature of natural history museum displays. Many of their dioramas, however, tell stories that are hopelessly out of date (for example, male chauvinist arrangements of lions or gorillas that actually represent bad science).[14] All museums tell a story or two in the form of the labels, but the custom has grown of using the exhibit labels to make politically correct points, sometimes with extreme clumsiness.

Gertrude Stein once described Ezra Pound as the 'village explainer'. It was meant as a put-down although it is easy to see it also as a compliment. We have created museums as institutions, not just to hold objects, but to explain them to ourselves. Museums love to explain things; they exist to explain things. Museums, fundamentally, *show* things, but that is never all they do and it is rarely enough. At one level, one might think that all this storytelling should be unnecessary. Surely all the museum should need to do is to display the objects – then the educated visitor will come and browse, seeing and taking away precisely what he or she cares to, or is able to. The insistently independent type will want no video or audio aids, will buy the guide book only on the way out, and has the capacity or interest to experience things for himself or herself. For one visitor it might be an intense intellectual experience in which, perhaps, the paintings on display are compared with others seen elsewhere, the imagery, the styles, the brushwork noted and analysed. For another visitor the experience might be like a visit to a cathedral of some foreign religion or a mountain seen for the first time – remote but beautiful and inspiring. At the other extreme is the fully integrated didactic experience with a tour guide (most likely via an earphone) who does the thinking for you. Objects have to be displayed (and all those labels have to be written) so as to accommodate all these different kinds of users, with messages both short and pithy (art museums and botanical gardens are best at this – some have no labels at all) and discursive and informative (natural history museums tend to go overboard here).

While an experience in which the museum object is simply 'abstracted' by the visitor wandering among the objects may be fine in theory, it is almost impossible in practice. It would be considered elitist to leave the matter there, because too many visitors would be excluded. Objects need explanation: reality must be reconstructed. The mere act of putting two paintings next to each other, let alone writing the labels or arranging the mounted animals in a diorama, involves a whole set of intellectual and aesthetic decisions that affect both the what and the how of the visitors' experience. Even if this were not so – if, for example, the object were something completely natural like an untouched part (if there is such a thing) of a national park or a Himalayan mountainscape – most visitors would still want to ask questions: What is that? Why is that? In a museum it is hard to leave questions unanswered, and that means that the questions have to be anticipated. And so the reality is reconstructed in a particular way, with particular labels and booklets – even the lighting is part of the craft or artifice of the experience. In the process the visitor is, paradoxically, both brought closer to the object and separated from it. The next best thing to 'untouched' is the invisible hand of someone you can trust. The distance in between is immense.

5
Who Collects What, and Why?

I cannot live without books.
Thomas Jefferson, letter to John Adams, 10 June 1815

If the heart and soul of a museum is its collections, then it must also be people, for people collect and people give (less commonly they sell) objects to museums. The worlds of private collecting and public collecting are inextricably bound together and the paradoxical pluses and minuses of museums all begin with the culture of collecting.

People collect objects for a multitude of reasons: to have, to preserve, to study, to teach, to give away. In the last century and a half, collecting of paintings and other *objets d'art* (fine or decorative), books, ethnography, historical artefacts, natural history specimens and technological materials has occurred on a scale far beyond anything our forebears could have imagined. The nineteenth century saw the rise of a prosperous middle class and, particularly, a very wealthy class aspiring to an upper class redefined on the basis of wealth and influence rather than family – in short, the Modern Way. Possessions became supremely important, and possessions of the intellectual rather than commercial world became most important of all. Art, not yachts and racehorses, became the *sine qua non* of the new millionaire classes (interestingly, the second and third generations often reverted to yachts and horses!).

Because of their origins in the world of commerce and technology, many nineteenth-century commercial barons turned society knights supported the growth of science museums and natural history museums. But clearly the *ne plus ultra* was art. Nowhere can one see this better illustrated than in Newport, Rhode Island, where a wealthy class aspiring to (or attempting to outdo) European nobility created 100-room 'cottages' built on grand pseudo-European plans and mostly furnished with reproductions or fanciful interpretations of European culture through the ages (less frequently, they imported the real thing).

Soon the race was on, not only to collect, but to collect in specific areas – for example, 'modern' paintings, which might mean anything after the Pre-Raphaelites. When Impressionist and Post-Impressionist works started to rise in esteem and popularity, becoming a target of collectors for aesthetic and snobbish reasons, the works of art naturally appreciated hugely in value. Further collecting in turn caused those values to soar in what continues today as a circle – whether vicious or charmed, I am not sure – until a painting that was unsold at Van Gogh's death in 1890 fetches nearly $100 million a century later.

The business of collecting, whether by individuals or institutions, seems to represent a primitive human trait. We collect for the power of possession, in order to preserve, in order to study, to encourage others and to explain, as an end in itself, for the thrill of the hunt and the 'kill'. Collecting often starts with an aesthetic reaction to a single object. The tour guides at the Winterthur Museum's almost obscenely large conglomeration of 83,000 objects and 200 reconstructed period rooms in Wilmington, Delaware, like to show you the first few ironstone plates that Henry Francis Du Pont bought as a student. Soon he had collectors all over the world buying for him, shipping them in by the crateload and then the shipload. Next, he collected the rooms and houses to put them in, the objects that went with them and so on. At Calke Abbey in Derbyshire, the National Trust has preserved the extravagant equivalent in the field of natural history: the Harpur-Crewe family's astonishing collection, especially of stuffed animals in glass cases.

Collecting is a grand passion with its own rhythms, disciplines and addictive behaviours regardless of the subject. Collecting involves acquisition. But one does not simply collect *more*; there is little point in having thirty copies of the same Hogarth engraving, unless one is interested in the mechanics of the printing process, revealed by endless comparisons among sister prints. Collecting only to have more is shallow. Any embryo collector soon sees the need to improve the collection, so as only to have the best examples. The central essence of collecting is to have 'a set' or 'the complete set'. This might be all the plastic geegaws put into breakfast cereal boxes by a particular company in 1990, or a painting from every one of Picasso's 'periods'. Indeed, one could very reasonably ask, what good is an incomplete set of anything? Whether one is conducting research on a single painter, a school of painters, or a family of butterflies, one needs the whole set. The goal of bringing together the authentic, complete set makes the world of collecting of any kind an exciting hunting ground in which one runs down the elusive last element – whether an actual hunt into remote landscapes for rare butterflies or orchids, or into galleries and auction houses, or via an armchair search through dealer and auction catalogues, the internet, books, family members and other secondary sources. For the serious collector there is the added attraction that the barriers between amateur and professional break down. One is admitted into the company of scholars and experts.

But while a great deal of the pleasure is in the chase, the all-consuming passion is the passion to possess. Collecting and collections are power; the greater power lies in possessions that few or no others can have. After the great explorers and collectors of the eighteenth and nineteenth centuries had set the way, the twentieth century took up the matter with zeal. Nothing is more indicative of a station in life than one's possessions, and nothing so quickly accords a new station than the acquisition of desirable cultural objects. The principle applies equally to nations as to individuals. Whatever the caricature – Midlands beer baron or computer-age tycoon – respectability is measured against some standard set in the novels of Edith Wharton.

Collecting gives power by association. Owning a painting by Degas brings one to a degree of one-ness with the artist that could never be achieved by owning every single book or film about the painter, or by visiting every museum displaying a work by him. To own even the simplest of hand tools from the seventeenth century, or a classic car, brings the possessor a unique connection to another age, another people. Antique guns and swords bestow a different kind of power, less subtle perhaps, more direct. One does not become a better painter, craftsman, driver or hunter by virtue of owning these objects, but the collection endows the collector with all sorts of authority, intellectual and aesthetic. I have already mentioned Dr Alfred Barnes and his extraordinary collection of paintings and sculpture now known as the Barnes Collection. Even though Barnes hired collectors to advise him, he still put a great deal of himself in his collection and the ways it was used. It was all his. Matisse was his friend. And if in his lifetime all that brought him less prestige than he hoped, that was probably because of his terrible personality and the fact that he was kicking against the pricks of Philadelphia society. In any other city, he might have been a star. Whether saint or sinner, refined blue-blood or upstart from the side of the tracks where museums are not usually built, collectors gain power through their collections. And at the appropriate scale the almost complete set of cigarette cards or beer cans carries the equivalent weight of a group of Cézannes or Hockneys.

The wonderful part of this power by association is that a great many people are motivated not simply by the urge to possess but by the desire to preserve and promote objects for the good of society. And this is surely the case with unwieldy things like large houses, ships or railway locomotives (indeed whole villages and railway systems) that could no longer be owned by individuals. Without this devotion of time, money and commitment, a great part of any cultural heritage would be lost. The same urge applies to natural features, whether landscapes (like Snowdonia or Yosemite) or individual species of animals and plants.

Collecting is addictive: one yearns for the next 'high' from a find. It has its own rules, especially if one is not very rich. I have wondered whether to collect when rich would be a bore – you simply send people out to buy for you. (But evidently not.) Many get a greater satisfaction in looking for the hidden bargain, never buying over a particular price, for example. Sooner or later, however, many collectors decide that a particular field is no longer giving them pleasure. I gave up collecting illustrated natural history books when the prices went sky high. Some collectors stop simply because their work is finished.

A friend of mine, the late Richard Freeman, was an English zoologist and authority on British natural history books.[15] Several times a week he walked a particular route through London visiting bookshops and particularly stalls in the open-air markets. Among his many passions was Darwin. His goal was to own a copy of every printing of every work by Charles Darwin. When I met him, at University College London in the early 1960s, he had a copy of everything except the first five thousandth printing of the first edition of *On the Origin of Species*. He knew where one could buy a copy for a small fortune, but persisted in his own search on his own terms. He found it in Foyles, then advertising itself as the world's largest bookshop. A copy had slipped through each of the many stages of sorting in the second-hand department, ending up on their shelves in Charing Cross Road. Perhaps no one had been able to imagine that it really was that rarest of all copies. So Richard bought it for a few shillings. His collection was complete.[16] One can guess the end of the story. After a few weeks' euphoria, he was miserable. Before long he had sold the lot to a library and started on a different collection.

How does one start again? The easy solution is to change fields: from the Impressionists to Abstract Expressionists, perhaps, or from Johnstone's Ironstone to early Wedgwood, or from Smurfs to Barbies. Another tactic is to get in first: to collect something that has not been collected before. But what would that be? An otherwise unknown artist, plastic cap pistols from the 1940s, toothpaste tubes, pop stars' underwear? No good! Someone has already got there first. Just about everything is being collected by somebody.

And so we come to the dilemmas and paradoxes. Suppose that over thirty years or so I have built up a collection of drawings. During those years, I have gained the most extraordinary pleasure from the task of bringing together this collection. I have found drawings in unlikely auctions and garage sales, some of my best buys have been for a fraction of what the pieces are now worth. I have become friends with important curators, a dozen major artists and a hundred major dealers and their hangers-on. I have truly felt the thrill of the chase, and the occasional bitter pangs of losing the quarry to someone else. I have experienced (in this dream) all the frustrations and joys of hunting and all the pleasures of ownership and of showing to my friends and to scholars and seeing pieces loaned to exhibitions here and there. Some are reproduced in books, perhaps there is even a book about my collection alone. In a very real sense I have also created wealth, because the set of my drawings is worth more than their sum as individual pieces.

If I were to donate those drawings to a museum, nobody would again have the pleasure or good fortune of adding any of these drawings to their own collections. Not only would these particular objects have been withdrawn from circulation, in the process of collecting otherwise unknown and unappreciated artists I will have driven up their prices. Rival collectors will have driven them

33

further. Putting them in an institution will increase the rarity of what is left outside. If the works had instead been sent to sale after my death (it is disconcerting not only to have created this mythical collection but also to have died!) my executors would have had to release the works slowly to avoid causing a crash in prices. This happened on a grand scale when Picasso died leaving literally thousands of works on paper in his studio.

The first dilemma of collecting is therefore that it is extremely selfish. No matter that a person's or an institution's idea of what makes a 'set' may be wildly individual and eccentric, since collectable items exist in finite numbers, the activity of collectors is bound to make future collecting harder and harder, especially if the items are then given to or bought by museums.

The second dilemma is that, as the concentration of important objects in museums causes prices to rise, and the pressure mounts to create new categories of 'collectables' the prices of which also rise, the result must be a progressive trivialization of the whole process. It is one thing to collect beer cans, it is quite another to beat their prices up to the point of absurdity, and it is ludicrous then to elevate them to some grand cultural status.

From dilemmas to paradoxes. While there may be a nobility and higher value in the objects themselves, the act of collecting and the sequelae of the collecting business have their distinctly dark sides. Were it not for the appalling scale of it all, it would be trite and redundant to write of the looting, killing, swindling, forgery and just plain theft that accompany so seemingly benign a passion as collecting art. Not all such mass villainy occurred in the distant past. We are regularly reminded that we still live under the shadow of the Second World War, when German, Russian *and* Allied armies swept across city and country alike, leaving behind misery, want, extortion, and looted homes and museums. The Nazi government of Germany looted a great proportion of Europe's art treasures during the Second World War.[17] In turn, the Russian government has consistently refused to return the works of art *it* looted during the Second World War from German institutions and individuals, considering it as booty and just compensation for the war's hardships. As recently as 1997, the Russian parliament voted again not to return these works and this decision was upheld by the Russian Constitutional Court in April 1998. While a few of these works have been exhibited and appear to be well enough conserved, most simply lie in storage, their condition unknown but unlikely to be improving.

With respect to the Second World War, we are reaching a fascinating period of transition. On the one hand, the original owners of looted art works are becoming very old or dying, making it harder to document claims on their behalf. On the other hand, those who benefited from all the looting are also dying, leaving families and institutions with the problem of dealing with (perhaps even discovering for the first time) an embarrassing but temptingly valuable legacy. As a whole generation that experienced the Second World War passes on, their families and governments are left with the problem of dealing with the loot. A classic case is the Quedlinberg Treasure, medieval church treasures encrusted in gold and jewels that turned up in a small town in Texas. Instead of being returned to their owner, or at least handed over to a responsible authority, the works only came to notice because they had been hawked around and sold in Europe.[18]

Neither have our institutions behaved as well as we might have hoped. Collectors and the auction houses and dealers that supply them have frequently turned a blind eye to the suspect – and often quite transparently so – provenance of paintings acquired during the 1940s. Museums in turn have been happy to shelter behind the supposed legitimacy of these transactions. The laws of most countries encode 200-year-old standards, according to which, to have kept a looted object for long enough (as little as five to ten years) bestows ownership. It is perhaps not surprising that a museum director, faced with questionable provenance of works that may well have been stolen by a member of the Allied forces ('liberated' is the dishonest euphemism) from Dresden in 1945, was quoted as wondering whether too much time has elapsed for any claim to be pursued legally.[19]

Sad to say, museums have history on their side. Were this not so, many of our museums would have significant gaps in their older collections. Where does one create a statute of limitations, as it were?

The situation took a new tack at the end of 1997 when two families claimed that paintings by Egon Schiele exhibited at the Museum of Modern Art in New York had been stolen by the Nazis prior to ending up in the Leopold Museum in Austria, the lender of the exhibition. A court ruling was obtained, temporarily keeping the paintings in New York instead of allowing them to travel back with the rest of the exhibit, in order to allow the case (which turned out to be far from clear-cut) to be examined.[20] Instead of at once admitting that such a claim required serious review, the museum community at first opposed this action. It argued that if US courts could impound 'suspect' objects for a trial of claims of legality, museums around the world would find it hard to get both individuals and sister institutions to lend them anything.[21] To which the man-on-the street might well add: amen. In April 1998 the first repercussions were felt when two Bonnard paintings from unnamed European private collections were withdrawn from a planned retrospective at the Museum of Modern Art in New York. In 1999, a similar hesitation concerning a Monet destined for a show in London caused *The Times* to whine in a headline: PUBLIC DENIED CHANCE TO SEE 'LOOTED' MONET. Since then museums all over the world have found a new resolve to search (years too late for most victims) for any possibly tainted works in their collections.

Surely the oldest profession in the world (despite competing claims) is that of thief. To mark the first day of the new millennium, thieves mimicking the film *The Thomas Crown Affair* stole a Cézanne from the Ashmolean Museum in Oxford. Ten years earlier, with similar flair, extremely clever thieves stole from the Isabella Stewart Gardner Museum in Boston immensely valuable paintings by Vermeer and Rembrandt. No possible market for such paintings could exist.[22] But none of them has been seen since. Apparently false newspaper reports aside, no ransoms have been demanded.[23] The list is too depressing to continue: every year thousands of other works and objects, less visibly, have been stolen from around the world. Possibly all these works now hang in the hidden vaults of perverse millionaires who could afford to pay the costs of such master crimes. Perhaps they are being used as collateral in high-stakes drug deals; or perhaps the thieves have found, as in O'Henry's story of the kidnapping of Red Chief, that they don't know what to do with their booty.[24] But when the guilty parties die, what will happen to the paintings? Will an embarrassed family quietly return them; will they be sold on to some other well-heeled crook? Or will they be quietly destroyed? Stay tuned.

Ironically, most of the paintings now so much enjoyed by visitors to Isabella Stewart Gardner's house-museum in Boston were bought for her by Bernard Berenson, who was hardly the most honest of traders. 'BB' and his wife Mary were almost gleeful about the way paintings were smuggled out of Italy:

> No one in Assisi was to know they had gone, except of course the friars. It is a fearful plot . . . Quite as exciting as the life of a smuggler of old in the caves on the coast . . . They take it to the Overseer at the Gallery here, packed in a large box, to get permission to export it. That is, they're supposed to, but in reality they take another picture, some worthless daub of the same size. The Inspector looks at it, and of course says they can do what they like with rubbish like that. He then gravely seals up the box and puts the mark on which serves to carry it through. But all the

time the box is cunningly made to open where he would never think of putting a seal, and they carry it home, open it in this secret way, and substitute the good picture for the bad.[25]

There is nothing glamorous or amusing about this. One could argue that Berenson 'saved' a lot of paintings from damp and neglect: 'I must tell you that I don't consider this wrong, because here in Italy the pictures are apt to go to ruin from carelessness.'[26] He would say that, wouldn't he? But Berenson's deliberate thefts and his immense profiteering from the authentication and sale of art scarcely do the museum world any credit. Unfortunately, the practice neither originated with Berenson nor died with him.

A trickier problem, also not unknown to Berenson, exists where those who have the authority to judge quality (through academic experience or institutional position) fail to keep themselves totally separate from the business of buying and selling. It can be a simple racket. Someone establishes a position as a scholar of artist X or period Y. He or she then buys lesser works the attribution of which is doubtful; hence the price is low. The scholar writes articles about these newly discovered works 'almost certainly from the hand of X', or perhaps they are placed in an exhibition or two. After this the drawings (or whatever) are worth a great deal more, so they can be sold on at a nice profit. One can do this quite honestly – or not. But in either case there is a problem: not just *caveat emptor* but, more to the point, *quis custodiet ipsos custodes*.

It is a major paradox, therefore, that the world of beauty and aesthetics should so often and so willingly resort to the tactics of barbarians. What should we, the public, feel when we visit museums that have divinely beautiful and fascinating objects obtained in dubious ways (which means most museums)?

Just behind looting comes forgery. As Van Gogh, Rembrandt and hundreds of other artists are no longer active, and are getting harder and harder to steal, pressure builds to produce them anyway. Some styles are easier to forge than others; it is often said, for example, that for every painting Corot produced, at least two are in the United States. Pressure on the authentic inevitably creates an industry of fakes. Those who devote themselves to the pursuit of the very best and the most 'real' assist unwittingly in the duping of others (and sometimes themselves). The need to possess, to fill the gap in the collection, can blind the person who would otherwise claim the one attribute necessary for any collector – the eye of experience and information. Auction houses have proved a particularly happy place for this to flourish. Of course, we all feel a grudging respect for the good forger. Not only does he or she prick the bubble of self-satisfaction in the wealthy collector (there is little point in forging things that potentially have no price), one feels a great, if puzzled, appreciation of the talent of a forger like Elmyr de Hory. One can readily imagine a collection – a whole museum in fact – being made of superb fakes, or of fakes by a particular hand. Sooner or later everything is collectable.

Some paintings that are not authentic are not forgeries either, of course – 'studio of' and 'school of' may describe a superb piece of art. No intrinsic value is lost when it turns out that a particular cherished work wasn't actually by Rembrandt's hand. The painting still *is*. Downright forgeries can claim no aesthetic value because they are in every sense *not*. But doubt, once sown, is a taint difficult to shake off. The claim that *perhaps* one of the most notorious paintings of recent years, the Van Gogh *Sunflowers* sold to a Japanese buyer, might be a fake, is probably just sour grapes. But whether by the hand of Van Gogh or not, it now sits in a bank vault as reclaimed collateral on a loan – possibly badly cared for and definitely not to be viewed.

The very worst kind of fakes are those objects that are produced openly and sold as 'collectables', the very notion of collectability being part of the deception. In terms of volume, the most collected items might turn out to be the ceramic plates, dolls, toys, coins and medals created specifically by clever businesses to be collected by the naive. Produced in large numbers and thereby having no rarity value, they appear to have little or no artistic value either. Their monetary value, in most cases, is like that of a new car – 20 per cent less the day after purchase. Some manufacturers of these objects have their own 'museums', which provide added authenticity. Such objects give a great number of people pleasure, which is fine as long as those people are not being duped into thinking that their collections will increase in value. Delightfully, there is an additional irony that these worthless objects do in fact enter serious museum collections. Most museums probably have in their basements sets of ceramic figurines or dolls donated by some patron, accepting them having been the price for getting some more traditionally collected item or a large cheque.

One could almost make a rule that anything labelled 'collector's item' is not worth collecting. But this would be wrong because, at the high end of this market, we find really fine porcelain, jewellery, guns, furniture, toys and – yes – paintings and sculpture, all made specifically to be collectable. These are not mass-produced but instead are the painstaking work of craftsmen and artists. And here we shade back to the world of museums. Many modern artists create works that for one reason or other, starting with size, could only be intended for those museums that buy works of art straight from the studio. Constantin Brancusi, for example, created works towards the end of his career that were explicitly destined to grace the museum that would inevitably be created for him. In the traditional way of things, there is something wrong with this practice. The collected object has not been authenticated by the passage of time and evolved opinion. The piece is 'good' only because it comes from an artist who has been pronounced 'good', and by the very fact of being in a museum collection – a circularity. While this is, on the surface, unobjectionable when the artist is 'genuinely' (whatever that means) a major artist, greater difficulties arise when the artist is unknown or emerging. The process then stands to interfere with that informal but rigorously effective agency by which the wheat is sorted from the chaff – the market-place of private collecting. And at the very least, the involvement of a museum is likely to inflate prices. Modern art, then, represents a minefield for the museum, the private collector and the serious artist alike.

It is a further paradox of museums and collecting that the barrier between the creation and original use of the object, and the authentication of its cultural value, is now so often transgressed. No one would argue that museums should always be stuck with 'old' and 'mainstream' art, and at the very least they should *exhibit* the works of emerging artists, whether unknown and worth knowing or fast in the eye of public interest. The question is: should museums, which are seen by everyone as the bastions (indeed the ultimate agents) of authenticity, *collect* in such areas? This is where the role of the objective, and above all, well-informed critic and independent media are paramount. Who else can be relied upon to tell us about the emperor's new clothes?

The principal paradox of collecting is that an exercise that depends on a free market produces a closed one. Slowly and inexorably, collectable objects of every kind are being removed from the realm of public transaction and locked up like the ice in Arctic glaciers. Most museum professionals consider this to be a good thing. I suggest that it may not invariably be the case.

6

Some Great Collections

The foundation of the whole glorious enterprise is the personal collection. Highly personal collections, by definition, make a perfect kind of whole, but this may only apply in a specific context and only for the original owners. There is particular magic in a collection made by a single person or family, even if it has been made with (or even for) them by someone else. Historic houses, great and small, in Britain represent this sort of collection, amassed over the centuries. Who could not love that eccentric collection at Calke Abbey (see page 29) or the perfect combination of house, contents, gardens and surrounding landscape at Sissinghurst Castle?

One of my favourite institutions is the Isabella Stewart Gardner Museum in Boston. Even though this collection of Old Masters was assembled in large part through the eye of Bernard Berenson (see page 37), Mrs Gardner's own personality everywhere comes through loud and clear and nowhere more than in the house itself, created to house the works and thereby to become a part of the whole. However, cruel things have been said about collections amassed by wealthy people under the guidance of expert advisers, and in putting one's collection on display one reveals rather more of oneself than may be wise. The collection of Walter and Leonore Annenberg, comprising Impressionist and Post-Impressionist paintings purchased largely between the years 1950 and 1980, contains some superb works, among which one might particularly point out Vuillard's *The Album* and Gauguin's *Siesta*.[27] But what of its status as a collection? Does the whole exceed the sum of the parts, as in the greatest personal collections? The art critic Edward Sozanski wrote:

Great collectors not only follow their intuition and their emotions, but illuminate the path for others. They take risks that only in retrospect seem like inevitable choices. Annenberg's collection, splendiferous though it may be in its particulars, settles for elegant bourgeois respectability ... What does this collection tell us about Walter Annenberg? That he favors pictures of upper-class women in domestic or leisure situations. That he likes flowers and gardens. And that green must be his favorite colour.[28]

Ouch! A tough world, this.

The Cone Collection, which forms the core of the Baltimore Museum of Art, takes us closer to the ideal of a personal collection. It was assembled by two sisters who between 1901 and 1949, travelled extensively to Paris and befriended artists such as Matisse and Picasso. They purchased an almost unbelievable set of works by Matisse, one or two per year, and eventually donated their whole collection (also including Picasso, Cézanne, Gauguin, Van Gogh and Renoir, as well as American artists, Middle Eastern decorative works and African and Asian art) to the city of Baltimore. Assembling this collection was a lifetime's work and a lifetime's pleasure. Giving it to the public made the works available to the public. The Museum of Art in turn had to raise the funds to build a wing to house them as their popularity rightly grew. Now they form a priceless archive as well as a delight to tourists.[29]

Among all personal collections, notable or notorious, the Herbert and Nannette F. Rothschild Collection stands apart as a superb example of a collection made as a labour of love and an expression of individual tastes.[30] It represents collecting at its very highest level but has only been exhibited twice: at the Rhode Island School of Design (1966) and at the Philadelphia Museum of Art and National Gallery of Art (1997). The collection consists largely of modern works on paper, starting with Léger, Kandinsky and de la Fresnaye, purchased one at a time as funds allowed (these were not the super-rich Rothschilds). This is a collection put together by two people, and their painter daughter Judith, who loved a particular kind of art and revelled in collecting it. One knows without asking that the works hung on the walls of their house. No other couple would have collected the same objects. Like all truly great collections, it perfectly reflects something of the Rothschilds' characters. On viewing it for the first time, I instantly wished I could have known them. They purchased works systematically over about twenty years, beginning in the 1950s. In the process they got to know the artists, the dealers, the environments – the real provenances – of the works. Their experiences fit together as a whole, as the collection itself does. The Rothschilds grew with their collection, always learning: a lifetime truly to envy.

The Rothschild collection also exemplifies the fragile integrity of such a personal endeavour. It is not the greatest didactic collection; it is in no way synoptic. If it were made the nucleus of a great small museum it would have to be augmented, and with the first additions the elegant integrity of the collection, its wholeness, would as quickly be lost. A family foundation is a very good home for such an intensely personal, idiosyncratic in the best sense, collection. But with the death of its creators, one can also imagine that the greater compliment to them and to the objects themselves would be to let the works back out into the market-place, to be realigned, put into different constellations and arrangements, by other art-loving, intelligent people. Or even buffoons. To live, in other words, rather than to be fossilized. The current director of the Foundation has stated that this is a possibility,[31] and it would be in keeping with the wishes of Judith Rothschild, who stipulated in her will (1993) that the collection should be kept together for only twenty-five years.

The Barnes Collection, in Merion, just outside Philadelphia, is equally idiosyncratic. For all that he fell short on personal charm, the late and generally unlamented Dr Albert C. Barnes assembled perhaps the greatest single collection of French paintings from the period 1880–1940. Not only did he early and unfashionably recognize the French masters,[32] he also collected neglected Americans such as Horace Pippin and Charles Demuth. Barnes formed his collection of paintings as an educational tool rather than as a typical museum. The integrity of the collection was essential to the particular style and approach of Barnes' teaching and still necessarily dominates the whole. He tackled the problem of presentation in the small Pennsylvania mansion in which the collection is displayed via a unique and not altogether crazy set of principles. In a scheme as eccentric as its owner, the paintings are crowded together on walls of mustard-ish linen together with a superb collection of African masks and American colonial wrought ironwork – the expression of a unique set of ideas. The result is so rich and overpowering that one has to punctuate a visit by pauses to come up for air, head spinning from the chaotic beauty and power of it all. This is not just a magnificent collection of works, it is Albert Barnes' collection; he and the collection are inseparable.[33] The Barnes Collection exists only in what one sees displayed. There will be no changes, there are no reserve collections or study collections in the back rooms.

The Barnes Collection also shows us some of the difficulties created when personal collections become public. Barnes (who made his money in patent medicines) created his institution as an educational trust. Over the years the educational mission became rather enfeebled, limited perhaps by Barnes' ideas and those of his equally inflexible assistant, Violet de Mazia. And certainly by Barnes' policies. He allowed no photographs of his works beyond a few fuzzy black-and-whites in his own books. No works were allowed to travel. Scholars were discouraged from visiting. *Visitors* were often discouraged from visiting. Then the money started to run out. The endowment was not enough, or had become not enough. The building needed work, starting with the installation of serious air conditioning. What had survived as the hobby of an eccentric was now, after his death, under pressure to become a public asset in line with its advantageous not-for-profit status. The new trustees grappled (often gracelessly) with the laborious, thankless and infinitely contentious job of turning the place into a regular museum in the face of almost iron-clad strictures in Barnes' will. After long court battles to make the terms of the will less rigid (to 'break' it, if you like), the collection was allowed a worldwide tour to raise funds to restore the building and build the endowment. Architectural miracles have hidden necessary structural and environmental improvements to the building and the collection has been re-hung – or rather replaced exactly as it was. Local courts still oscillate between allowing regular hours and restricting them to the original two and a half days a week and 300 visitors per day. One of the problems – the absence of parking, especially for buses, in a quiet suburban neighbourhood – continues to nurture a festering local resistance to the institution that tries to keep pace with the spreading of its international reputation.

Life tending always to maximum contrariness, the 'new' Barnes is punished and vilified for doing what it needed to do earlier – change the mission, use the resources, publish books, sell T-shirts, postcards and CD-ROMs, and support itself, thereby becoming more open to the public whose tax laws help make its continued existence possible. The Barnes might have remained small and private, but it lacked the resource to do that and a public cultural imperative for which it was unprepared required that its glories be patent to a wider public. At last report it was still in deep financial trouble, despite being worth (conservatively) billions.

This leads us, perhaps, to the example of the Barbier-Mueller Collection of Geneva, which is worth mentioning because it exists independently of any public institution. There is no building and no permanent exhibits. Instead, a world-class collection of ethnographic objects exists principally to be formed and re-formed into travelling exhibitions to be sent around the world.

7

From Individual to Institution

I cannot say I shall be happy to have it in my power to comply with your
request by sending you the bodies of my Pheasants, but expect that it will
not be long before they will compose a part of your Museum, as they all
appear to be drooping.

George Washington, letter to Charles Willson Peale, 9 January 1787

Each fancies . . . that it is the business of somebody else to look after this
or that for him; and so, by the same notion being entertained by all sepa-
rately, the common cause imperceptibly decays.

Thucydides, *The History of the Peloponnesian War*, 5th century BC

Every properly documented painting comes with its provenance –
a list of owners, of places exhibited, and of books and catalogues
where it is mentioned. A record of authenticity, this is a kind of living document, beginning with the name of the artist and growing
with each change of owner and each significant exhibition or cita-
tion. It is the work's pedigree, a story told in names and places,
from artist to artist's family member perhaps, a dealer, a banker, a
collector. For more and more objects, the list is now closed, complete except for notations about matters such as exhibitions, loans
and conservation. The object will change hands no more because
the list ends with the name of a museum.

Every year a new cohort of hundreds of thousands of cultural
objects passes from private to semi-public ownership, from the
fluidity of the market-place to the permanence of the institution.
This amounts to an enormous transfer of wealth and fosters a
huge museum industry: acquiring, displaying, teaching, advertising, merchandising, building and, above all, fund-raising.

Not all great collections end up in museums, however. For

example, we will never be able to visit a Dora Mar-Picasso Museum in Paris. Picasso's mistress Dora Mar assiduously collected every scrap of material from her life with the artist, from paintings to doodles on napkins and little wire figures twisted from the seals of wine bottles. She made no will and the collection was dispersed at auction. Predictably, almost all public accounts have bemoaned the fact that the collection could not be kept together as its own museum. *Another* museum.

There have been great collections from antiquity onwards, but the public museum is really a twentieth-century phenomenon – the Ashmolean Museum of the University of Oxford, open to the public from its inception in 1683, and the British Museum (1753) are notable exceptions. While arising in the seventeenth century, museums open to the public, owned by local government or a not-for-profit independent entity – as opposed to a great house of royalty or nobility, church or university – really flowered with the increase of private affluence of late nineteenth-century and early twentieth-century collectors and a growing middle-class interest in material culture.

In Britain most museums are publicly owned and operated. The Museums Acts of 1845 and 1850 gave authority for local councils to found and maintain public museums and the Museums and Gymnasiums Act of 1891 empowered them to charge a half-penny tax to support collections of archaeological and general local interest. There is a growing movement now to transfer such local authority museums to the custody of private trusts.

In the twentieth century, collecting rose to the level of a major industry and, sufficient time having passed for many of the great early collectors to have died (and universally failed to take their earthly treasures with them), these collections have increasingly passed into the holdings of museums large and small. The result has been the creation or enlargement of a large number of institutions all managed for the public good, even if we cannot afford them.

Equally, two factors – rising prices and an increasing population of enthusiastic collectors in every part of society – may be said to have reduced our discrimination (at the most generous we might say 'broadened our horizons') with respect to what represents a culturally valuable collection – that is, one we presume the public wants to 'own'. Not only have collections of the traditional categories of items – paintings, ceramics, sculpture, prints, drawings, for example – increased, but whole new categories have arisen or been created. Photography is an obvious example, but I have in mind also the rise of museums and private collections having to do with everything from soup tureens to jelly moulds and McDonald's plastic toys. Almost any list one could make of subjects apparently too esoteric (or absurd) to be the subject of a museum will immediately be trumped. In recent years we have seen, for example, a medical leech museum, a museum of Spam, 'a museum of culinary history and alimentation', and one for the former speaker of the House of Commons, Betty Boothroyd.[34] At the same time, one is hard pressed to prove that none of these is totally lacking in redeeming social interest.

High culture or low, all this activity involves amassing and transferring huge numbers of items to the responsibility of 'public' stewardship and ownership. There is, of course, a deeply principled aspect to this transfer of the ownership of the objects of civilization – sublime or ridiculous – out of private hands. Parallel to the individual collector's passion there exists a common public drive, often expressed as a public *right*, to 'own' works of art and other cultural objects. It derives in part from a deeply rooted feeling that the public has, in every legalistic as well as philosophical sense, an 'interest' in the materials of culture. This in turn reflects the success of museums in educating the public about culture and cultural objects, particularly paintings and historical materials. As culture is no longer the sole province of the wealthy few, the private ownership of great works seems, in this post-Marxian world, less and less politically and philosophically appropriate. Terms such as 'cultural heritage' and 'patrimony' now acquire special meaning, as does the constantly evoked concept of 'public trust' and something of a parallel *distrust* of wealthy (or lucky) owners of important collections. In the case of painters like Van Gogh, all this produces a superb irony. First he could not sell his works because no one was interested, then prices went sky-high; now the public is almost unnaturally preoccupied by his work, and the notion of any one of them being bought and sold on the open market is anathema. Next to this in irony is the slightly absurd xenophobia expressed in public resentment in Britain or the USA over the sale of one of 'our' French paintings to a Japanese buyer.

The matter of the public's interest (using the word in a legal sense) in works of art, science and material culture is rarely invoked openly except when an institution lacks the funds necessary to acquire a particular object. Special public appeals then have to be made and justified (as happens almost every week in Britain as an impoverished family sells part of a cultural legacy). For many such objects a strong case can be made for public rather than private ownership. This applies especially to the protection of the objects in their original setting – particularly in the case of houses and ships, which necessarily always exist in the public eye and where the loss would be directly experienced by many. Other whole classes of objects may be deemed, by general public consensus, to be wholly beyond the realm (beyond the pale) of private ownership and the possibility of private profit. Here the most obvious case would be materials relating to the Holocaust or slavery but the concept has been applied to any object of transcendent importance.[35]

The concept of pubic interest is also often applied reactively, not so much when a collection becomes available to pass from private to public hands, but the reverse – museum de-accessions. For example, in 1997 when the Historical Society of Pennsylvania recently proposed to sell some of its collection of artefacts, an editorial in the *Philadelphia Inquirer* rumbled:

> the court, using its considerable discretion here, should order that every effort be made to keep the artefacts in the public domain . . . The people of Philadelphia are entitled to keep the treasures of their history intact and in the city.[36]

The courts might in fact be able to make such an order, but are not capable of ordering that someone provide the funds.

The transfer of cultural materials from private/individual to semi-public institutional ownership represents an often unrecognized movement towards the effective socialization of cultural assets. It is ironic, therefore, that it so often depends upon a fiscal advantage being given to the sorts of wealthy people who own large valuable collections and other assets. In the United States, apart from the genuine impulse towards philanthropy on the part of many enlightened individuals, foundations and corporations, collections are donated to museums because the American government has made it financially advantageous to donate collections to museums and to create new museums. In Britain public funds are frequently used to purchase for museums works of art that have been accepted by the Treasury in lieu of estate taxes, but far more collections revert to the market-place. On both sides of the Atlantic, large and small collections steadily pass to institutional ownership. As a result, I can be safe in stating that at no time in history have so many cultural objects entered the care – the vaults, really – of institutions. And the process is accelerating, at the inevitable cost of a decrease in average quality. Another paradox: it is more than a little disingenuous for the museum community to argue that one of the advantages of the tax system is that it allows them to obtain works they could never afford on the open market, when the same system keeps works *off* the market and raises the cost of what remains.

The unresolved, perhaps unresolvable, issue about the public's 'right' to own or to control cultural objects often brings different 'rights' into conflict. Many groups (for example, North American Indians) have objected strongly to the collecting, either public or private, of their private cultural objects and the callously indifferent public exhibition (or study) of sacred objects and symbols meant only for the eyes of an inner few, if anyone. Most offensive of all is the collecting of grave objects and skeletons, hence the return of a Ghost Dance shirt from Glasgow's Kelvingrove Museum in 1999. It used to be argued that collecting was acceptable if the burial was 'pre-contact'. The general public sense is that this is no longer so, and rightly. There is a nice passage in the novel *Talking God* by Tony Hillerman, in which an anthropologist (Caucasian) receives a package containing the bones of her grandparents, dug up from a cemetery, and offered in exchange for two Native American skeletons from the Smithsonian.[37] Touché.

Even so, there is a persistent, nagging, cultural imperialism to the following effect: many of these objects may well have been made for sacred or otherwise private purposes and, indeed, deliberately to be disposed of, not kept. But our need to know, to understand and to value, overrides the original purposes. You, the descendants of the makers, and we, the outsiders, should now stand side by side in studying, displaying and appreciating them. In our culture, in other words, nothing may be truly our own. What rights to privacy do our forebears then have? Must patrimony become currency?

In one respect I find myself sympathetic to the various peoples who have wanted their cultural items to follow their intended course and return to nature. As a scholar, I can also argue the opposite case for the urge to know. For example, in 1996 a now notorious human skeleton was dug out of a bank of the Columbia River in Washington State. 'Kennewick Man' turned out to be of outstanding scientific importance, being not only very old – 9300 years (among the oldest human skeletons in North America) – but also arguably showing Caucasian characteristics and a lack of American Indian features. Local Umatilla Indian people, who have not been in the region long enough to have an ancestral claim on the skeleton (or, if we grant its apparently non-Indian features, a genetic claim), demanded that it immediately be turned over to them for reburial under the auspices of the Native American Graves Protection and Repatriation Act. They denied that it should be studied. In this case, since no one can claim ownership either legally on the grounds that it is a fossil or mineral (the skeleton was found on Federal land), or genealogically, whose interests are stronger? Native American or world scientific? If it were my ancestor, even my grandfather, and he turned out to be scientifically interesting, I would have no objection at all to study of the remains or the deposition in a museum. The study of my grandfather's remains would contain no coded insult to my kin. At least, I think not.

All this is related to the even more difficult issue (because of the number of items involved) of repatriation of cultural objects of broader artistic, cultural and national scope. The flagship issue here is the Elgin Marbles, but one might equally consider all the works taken by Napoleon from Egypt. There is no simple answer to these problems, whose origins lie in deals long forgotten and practices no longer tolerated (or even legal). However, one can consider what would happen if national repatriation were carried to its logical extreme, all past contracts were repudiated, and everything were back *in situ*. All Egyptian antiquities would be in Egypt, for example, all Renoirs would be in France, all Rothkos in America, all Turners in England, and all *Archaeopteryx* fossils in Germany. And we would all be the poorer. In between the extremes is some form or other of the present chaos. The situation cannot be resolved by the application of broad, blind principles but requires an item by item discussion.

When all is said and done, despite nagging worries, of course public stewardship by museums is essential. It offers the most professional way of preserving and caring for our cultural treasures. There is no gainsaying that institutions save our present and past cultures. Indeed, left to themselves, private collectors, however well-intentioned, may do more harm than good. However, private or public, there is no point in laying up treasures on earth in institutions whose long-term prospects we cannot guarantee.

8

The Consequences of Size

There are stored in the cellars of the Museum immense collections of
Fishes and Reptiles which have never been of use to anyone except the
assistants in charge of them. A very large part of this material, collected
and maintained at great expense, ceases after a time to be of value for
scientific purposes, and every year we are obliged to throw away as
absolutely worthless a large number of specimens.

Alexander Agassiz, *Annual Report of the Museum of Comparative
Zoology*, Harvard College, 1883–84

Agassiz (given the quote above) evidently had not heard the story
of the University of Oxford's dodo. In 1755, a survey of the collections of the Ashmolean Museum and the anatomy department
showed that many older specimens were spoiled by insect infesta-
tions, damp and all the other problems affecting the genre. Large
numbers were burnt. Legend has it that someone plucked from
the bonfire the remains of Oxford's dodo – which had been one of
the few live specimens brought to Europe in the early 1600s. At the
time no one was sure the species was extinct. Now these remains
are only one of two or three surviving specimens of the dodo anywhere in the world's museums (all other remains being sub-fossils
collected in the 1880s). The Oxford dodo, along with a painting
from 1652, was displayed in the new museum built in 1860, where
they became the favourites of a mathematics don, Charles Dodg-
son, and his young friends, Alice Liddell and her sisters, and were
later immortalized in *Alice in Wonderland*. Currently, molecular
biologists are extracting DNA from the mummified skin. Perhaps
that is what people mean when they say 'the rest is history'.

Without collections, a museum either does not exist or it exists only as a shadowy world of video screens and 'entertainment concepts': all very useful no doubt, but useful in a different way. The Guggenheim Museum in Bilbao and the Tate Modern in London are superb buildings, but if the works on display are poor, who – in the long term – will come? For any museum, travelling blockbuster exhibits, weekend children's programmes, or daily guided tours may be wonderful, but not without the collections themselves. Civic pride will not produce consistent queues at the box office, nor will celebrity guest appearances. Lunchtime concerts and evening films may help, but all depend upon a base: the works. The only possible exception to this rule concerns the gift shop. For many years, the gift shop of the Museum of Northern Arizona in Flagstaff was a major draw in part because of its superb inventory of American Indian (particularly Navaho) jewellery. Somewhere there may be a terribly second-rate museum that survives, thronged with visitors, solely because of a superb gift shop. But I am not sure.

Oppositely, many things not directly related to the collections can serve to act as a barrier to going to a museum: the forbidding façades of so many of our museums, the rudeness of the guards at — (fill in the blank), the problems of parking (everywhere), a dangerous neighbourhood, the cost. All these are problems that can be solved. But if the collections of the museum are not superb, people will not visit. And without an audience, the greatest collections in the world are empty in every sense. Advertisements for the Victoria & Albert Museum that once touted 'an ace café with quite a nice museum attached' were apparently whimsical!

Not surprisingly, the commonest measure of a museum's greatness is not the quality of its holdings but the quantity. Size is almost always a matter of glorification today. No one would be happy if the largest art collection in London were the Courtauld Collection. The City of New York is presumably happier that its largest museum is the size of the Metropolitan than it would be were it the size of the Frick Collection. In his turn, Childs Frick presumably was happier with that house on Fifth Avenue than he would have been with a 'trinity' in Greenwich Village. Henry Francis Du Pont really loved his nearly 200 rooms and 83,000 objects, from wainscoting to chamber pots, at Winterthur. Six rooms that were more truly authentic and original would not have satisfied. No one dreamt of putting the Tate Modern in a *small* power station.

There is a common life history to most museums. They either start like the British Museum or the collections at Oxford, with the gift of an obsessive collector – 80,000 objects from Sir Hans Sloane began the British Museum in 1759, the huge collections of the Tradescants and Elias Ashmole did the same for Oxford (1683) – or they start with small collections and a big idea. The Museum of Modern Art in New York began with eight drawings and a single print plus a driving mission to explain modern art in a city already well endowed in more traditional fields of art. In the same way, any private collection begins with those first few purchases for the living room and library. At first, the majority of the objects are in daily use/display; accessibility is high. In many smaller museums there still continue to be no extensive collections beyond what you see – the house and its furnishings, the ship, the objects in cases and paintings on the walls. In most institutions, however, as a result of seemingly inexorable growth, what is displayed comes to represent only a fraction of the entire holding. The other collections are usually carefully and meticulously catalogued and equally meticulously stored in appropriate conditions – or perhaps jammed into cardboard boxes and placed in attics and basements where 'moth and rust doth corrupt'.

Museums attract collections. For many people it is a matter of pride that Aunt Effie's Venetian glass is in the local historical museum, together with the photograph of great-grandfather mowing where they built the shopping mall. Some are donated because people think of museums as high-class attics where one's own things can be stored, with the added attraction of a tax break for the donation. 'After all, we couldn't throw them away or sell them, now could we?' Donations are not easily turned aside when the objects come with a cheque – or even *might* come with a cheque. To get one or two superb objects from a donor one may have to accept a hundred lesser ones. In fact, the vast majority of collectors honourably donate their collections to local museums with the hope and expectation that they are thereby making something useful available to the citizens of that region.

People who collect are drawn to museums and museums cultivate people who collect, angling for a donation of that collection of Nilotic masks, those Indonesian butterflies, the early photographs, the modern paintings. It takes iron discipline to do otherwise. A museum may want that collection of masks equally whether it has no masks at present or already has many and wants more. In collecting, as elsewhere, nothing succeeds like success. People give objects, often whole collections, to institutions that already have wonderful collections. For example, in the late 1990s any number of institutions lusted after the art collection of Walter and Leonore Annenberg, with its wonderful Gauguins, Cézannes and Renoirs. After (presumably) much thought and (doubtless) much manoeuvring on all sides, the Annenbergs gave their collection to the Metropolitan Museum of Art. Not to some worthy institution in which it would have been a jewel, a seed from which much more might grow, not to the Philadelphia Museum of Art where it would have made a good collection of nineteenth-century paintings great, but to the largest art museum in the country which needed it like they needed a statue of Sylvester Stallone.

Museums actively seek new collections almost as a duty because, by adding to their collections, they obviously preserve more of our cultural patrimony. So museums pro-actively add to their existing collections by purchase, exchange or (where appropriate) by sending out expeditions. There was a major surge in acquisitions for many museums in the 1960s and 1970s.[38]

In principle, the public gains three advantages from such acquisition of our cultural heritage: the collection is transferred to public ownership or stewardship, the collection is held together as a unit, and the objects become much more accessible. However, I suggest that placing objects in large institutions does not in itself guarantee increased public access. Unfortunately, quite to the contrary: the overwhelming majority of objects in a large museum are rarely if ever seen by the public. There are too many such objects. Gifts of further collections to institutions may not be doing either the institution or the public a service after all. The addition of a large collection to an institution's holdings may represent a burden as much as an opportunity for all concerned. Furthermore, the wholesale transfer of collections of every kind of cultural objects to semi-public institutions is surely encouraged by the very existence of so many institutions, creating a positive upward spiral of cause and effect.

All this growth ought to be a Good Thing. If objects are information, no institution can ever have enough – the National Maritime Museum could scarcely have too many ships, for example. However, the paradox of size in the case of collections is that more is not always better when it comes to working within a coherent business plan matching ambitions to resources. As collections grow, they become like an iceberg, the bulk of which is mostly unseen, and therein lies the source of a whole range of problems, both for the institution and for the public.

The obvious problems of growth include the cost of maintenance, insurance, costs of buildings, curation and conservation and so on. There are also considerable opportunity costs, as more of the building is devoted to storage of objects, as more of the staff and more of the budget are devoted to maintaining objects, less is available for public programming. These are material difficulties and for some few institutions and private individuals they represent no obstacle at all: money can be found. For many other collections these fiscal problems are overwhelming, but even so they are – in the cosmic realm of worth where institutions like to imagine themselves – trivial.

Underlying these mere fiscal problems are other, perhaps far more serious, sequelae of collection growth. The first consequence may be termed 'the invisible collections'. By placing more and more of the material objects of our culture into 'public' museums we actually take them further and further from our own experience: the bigger the museum becomes, the more inaccessible the majority of its collections must inevitably be. Therefore collections that were added to the institution with the explicit or implicit goal of making them accessible to the public, are hidden away. At least, one can say they are safe, but to what purpose?

This leads to the second consequence of growth: the change of institutional function from action to archive. As their collections grow, institutions change in an important way. Many large museums begin to acquire objects, either deliberately or by force of circumstance, *without ever intending to display them to the public*, but rather to have and hold an archive – implicitly or explicitly for scholarly research, or simply to preserve for the future. Such museums tend to develop their collections not simply into a better reserve for future exhibitions or for loan, but as 'study collections'. This is partly driven by necessity, for not all the objects that have been donated or bought over the years are of exhibit quality. Mostly this growth results from a drive to establish reference resources – examples of all the states of printing in the engravings of Dürer or Rembrandt, or all the species of butterflies in Costa Rica. In turn, when collections grow, the libraries and other supporting functions of the institutions grow too, until they also become a major resource for the scholar.

Perhaps least understood by the public is that, in most museums, the curators actively collect in their own field of specialization. To the scholar, the more objects the more the scholarly information. The reason for this is that, parallel to the 'reconstruction of reality' that museums engage in, there is also a 'reinterpretation of reality'. The scholars may be members of the museum's staff, or from the wider world of scholarship beyond. The larger the museum, the more likely it is that a curator will have time for her or his research in addition to all the other duties. Ideally, every curator has both scholarly training and credentials and has the opportunity to contribute further to the field. (Not surprisingly, when resources are tight, research is often the first item to be sacrificed.) This work is carried out behind the scenes, behind those doors through which the public may not pass but which sometimes are left invitingly open to reveal a glimpse of the other half of the museum – thousands of objects in ordered rows, or workshops, and men and women engaged in tasks whose meaning is obscure. In many museums there is a move to open up these barriers with glass walls and open storage areas. Many studying the collections are not museum staff, nor university types working on their next book. They are serious-minded enthusiasts from every walk of life engaged in self-directed learning and who represent an enormous national resource in terms of knowledge in areas such as local and regional social history, archaeology, natural history, palaeontology, arts and crafts, technology and manufacturing.

On the grand scale, museum collections seek to embrace the whole history of art and material culture and of life on earth. This function of museums as an archive or repository is a vital one as it feeds the scholarly study of every aspect of culture. The museum business is not simply a matter of taking care of objects – it is all about using them. Our interpretations of objects change all the time as learning progresses. For example, it used to be thought that the very biggest dinosaurs, such as *Brontosaurus*, were so large that they had to live partially floating in swamps. Careful study of the bones of dinosaurs shows that this is wrong, some were actually quite mobile. Study of the microscopic structure of the bones shows us that they had advanced physiology – they were warm-blooded like mammals. In art, much is being made of the fact that artists such as Vermeer used the camera lucida in composing their paintings, a fact revealed by close study of the paintings themselves. X-rays of paintings show how the artist developed a picture, often changing his or her mind.

There is always something new to learn or reinterpret. In these careful studies, one often needs suites of objects. One Acheulean hand axe is an impressive testimony to an ancient culture and technology; a suite of hand axes, even broken ones, can tell us much more about exactly how they were made. A series of different copies of the same engraving by Dürer or Mary Cassatt tells us a huge amount about the development both of the particular image and the artist's intentions. For all these reasons of interpreting reality, museums need huge comparative collections.

Such scholarly uses of collections are essential because they expand our knowledge about our past and present. Scholarship is a crucial function for the museum community, if not necessarily for every museum. Museums promote the scholar, forming essential resources for many scholars in the humanistic, social science and scientific subjects. We value such study almost as highly as we value the objects themselves. After all, what good is a cultural heritage unless it is analysed and explained? What good is scholarship if its basic material resources are missing?

The collections of even the smallest museum have some potential for study. Having spent part of my career as a research scientist, working on museum collections and adding to them where possible, I am well placed to appreciate this role for museums. As a director, I want my collections to be used and am keen to provide every kind of support for access to the collections, starting with a digital database of information that can be read by anyone. But, if

I step aside and look at this central role of so many of our museums, great and small, from outside the institutional nest, an odd paradox appears. Museums are part of the scholarly industry, but principally as providers of and carers for the raw material. Museum (and library) staffs include scholars, but just as 99 per cent of a museums collections are in the research stores, so 99 per cent of a museum's scholarly users are outside the institutions. Many users are in universities and research institutes that, for the most part, do not maintain collections (the great old universities like Oxford and Harvard being the exception rather than the rule). While some universities are striving to establish new museums to add to their academic credentials, others that have amassed teaching collections are often trying hard to disperse them to someone else's museums to be cared for. Again, this should all be a wonderful sign of the strength of museums and should define a crucial role for them. But who will pay the bills?

Scholarly users of museum collections expect to have free access. Museums, to put it bluntly, have a product they cannot afford to 'make' and customers who do not pay. Museums are service providers without adequate subsidy. So far, no one has worked out a strategic plan for the whole sector that can sustain it over the long term, although a Regional Museums Task Force, set up in England in 2001, is the first major step down this long road.[39] Meanwhile, everybody, museum curators and scholarly users alike, is happy if the collections grow and grow.

As collections grow, once a critical point is passed, the institution is forced into a dichotomy of function between the 'working collections' upon which the public displays are based and the 'study/reserve collections'. The working collection becomes more and more the realm of public education and entertainment and the reserve collections, by contrast, become the preserve of a few (critics would say an elite few). It is impossible to accommodate both functions in the public spaces and the two collections have to be managed differently, especially with respect to growth and resources. John Edward Gray, describing the British Museum in 1864, saw this problem clearly:

> What the largest class of visitors, the general public, wants, is a collection of the more interesting objects so arranged as to afford the greatest possible amount of information in a moderate space . . . on the other hand, the scientific student requires to have under his eyes and in his hands the most complete collection that can be brought together . . . In a futile attempt to combine these two purposes in one consecutive arrangement, the modern museum entirely fails in both particulars.[40]

The result is the dual museum: one part for the public and the other, behind closed doors, for the scholar.

Natural history museums present a special case here. Their collections exist almost entirely for study and research and often number in the millions of specimens. Such collections are almost never interconnected with the public displays. In fact, in most natural history museums the number of objects on view has actually declined in recent years as cluttered Victorian synoptic displays are replaced with lean, modern, didactic ones. The exhibited specimens are often not the 'prizes' of the collection in the way that an art museum's are. When exhibit specimens are no longer used in public display it is often hard to know what to do with them. These 'excess' specimens often are not of research quality and go into a special kind of limbo – faded birds without proper labels, duplicate specimens of minerals, elephant skulls too large to fit in the regular storage cabinets, and all those trophy heads of African and Asian mammals that lack data but, being on the endangered species list, cannot be disposed of. Another collection, that is, that no one wants but no one knows what to do with.

At first sight, one would imagine that the larger and more diverse the resources of an institution, the greater would be its flexibility. An institution devoted at first to furniture could surely do more and better work in reaching out to a broader public if it embraced the fine arts, or African masks, or even plastic toys or Barbie dolls? Perhaps this kind of flexibility does grow in principle, but in practice growth brings such resource problems that flexibility and innovation in programming – essential to direct interaction with the public – may be lost in the struggle simply to keep the doors open.

As functions change, one asks again: whose museum is this? The scholarly function, except in the case of the great national and university museums, rarely, if ever, depends upon an explicit mandate or even an implicit social contract with the supporting public. The situation is captured in the problem of matching resources with aims. 'Think globally: act locally' is fine as a byword for the environment; for museums it is something of a disaster. Except for a few in the largest cities, like London, Washington and New York, most museums are truly local museums. Public subsidy and private philanthropy are focused within a small geographical region – just beyond which is another city with its own institutions vying for support. New Yorkers do not give to Los Angeles institutions in large numbers, nor Londoners to Manchester, Glaswegians to York, and so on. The fate of too many museums is to grow to such a size that their collections constitute a resource of national or international importance while they are still supported on this local base. When I was president of the Academy of Natural Sciences, I found that people in Philadelphia might be surprised that we had some 25 million specimens and an international research programme, while scholarly colleagues around the country and abroad might not know (or care) that the institution supported a major public museum.

There is a problem, therefore, of matching both the size of the resource base and also the appropriateness of the expenditures to the public interest. No one has yet solved this problem of how to fund essentially local museums that maintain collections of major regional, national and international scope, although in Britain the National Heritage Lottery Fund and the Designated Collections Scheme have gone a considerable way in this direction. Most tax-payers and most individual members and donors are probably happy to support (within reason) their local museums in keeping and using for public purposes all the collections that are donated or purchased. They probably would be less happy if they knew how little access the public had to 90 per cent of those holdings. It is much easier to attract donors to support the public education and entertainment activities of our museums than a scholarly research function. Indeed, one often gets the feeling that the public who are asked to support the whole venture are justified in wondering whether, if the museum is short of money for public programmes, guards, children's programmes and better parking, the tail might not be wagging the dog.

The last problem is perhaps the hardest to address. Museums are institutions whose whole existence has been defined around the acquisition and care of collections. There is no comparable ethic for critical review and editing of collections. As time goes by, museum collections come to contain a larger and larger number of objects that never have been widely used and are no longer needed. But all must be maintained, at considerable cost.

The paradox of size, therefore, is that growth, which implies success, brings huge (largely hidden) costs, both fiscal and conceptual. In its simplest form, the paradox is that public use of the collections begins to take second place to the fact of the collections. This curious progression affects most museums, but not all. A museum like the Kimbell (see page 16) or, even more so, an historic house like Chatsworth, has a great advantage, the Kimbell because it is determined to change without growing, and Chatsworth because it doesn't have to do either.

9
Must Everything be Saved?

Can we ever have too much of a good thing?
Cervantes, *Don Quixote de la Mancha*, 1605–15

It is through art, and through art only, that we can realize our perfection.
Oscar Wilde, *The Critic as Artist*, 1890

All art is quite useless.
Oscar Wilde: *The Picture of Dorian Gray*, 1891

That *all* the materials of our cultures have become important, and that collecting has become both a major international pastime[41] and an industry, can be seen from the fact that in 1997 a McDonald's Black History Month Happy Meal box (presumably minus the original food contents) sold for $1200 and the associated colouring book for $1800.[42] To anyone who asks for the underlying principles, there is a simple answer: 'Paintings, sculptures, pottery, quilts and samplers, household utensils, silver and pewter, dolls, furniture and artisans' tools, are as susceptible to analysis and interpretations [of cultural history] as written texts.'[43] Wise words, but is all information of equal worth? Today, it seems that the worth of what is to be saved is almost too politically complex an issue to be discussed, with the result that the trivial and the sublime are treated together.

Barbie dolls make a fine example. Barbie dolls could scarcely be more trivial in any sense: mass-produced, distinctly low-brow, and anatomically improbable. Yet Barbie is now over forty, and has evolved over the years of her manufacture, so now scholars write serious dissertations on the doll in which they have found fascinating cultural commentary and meaning in the changes of body proportions, fashions, accessories, etc.[44] Barbie was among the first to be examined this way; others have followed. Barbie turns out to be a true cultural phenomenon and a fascinating if distorted reflection of our times; it would be a loss if no Barbie dolls were to be preserved for future generations. How *much* of a loss it would be if no Barbies were preserved for posterity is something that no scholar would stoop to consider. And since Barbie has now been popular with three generations of young girls, she has a claim upon posterity.

Let us grant the worth of Barbie.[45] But what about all the other kinds of plastic toys, what about beer cans and matchbooks? Must we collect them all – every kind of doll, in case other models turn out to be more informative than Barbie – every kind of manufactured object, the work of everyone who classes himself as an artist, an artisan, a collector? What then?[46] What, for example, shall we make of John and Eleanor Larson of Colusa, California, who have a collection of 1500 McDonald's paper tray liners?[47]

Once one embarks on collecting, there is no knowing where to stop, because the greatest curse is not knowing what is or will be important. There is an imperative to collect. As each decade passes, another cohort of objects becomes historically/culturally important. Staff at English Heritage – the custodians of places like Stonehenge – are seriously reviewing modern buildings (airfield installations, for example) remaining from the Second World War and similar artefacts from the Cold War. Suddenly 1960s tower blocks and 1970s manufacturing sites are worth study and preservation. Modern computers are already museum pieces (remember the Sinclair ZX and the Commodore?).

How can we be sure we get all this right – preserving what is worth preserving and letting the rest go? It is like the old joke about the cost of advertising: businesses know that half their money spent on advertising is wasted, they just don't know which half. Half of what we have collected and now so carefully conserve might be worthless; but we cannot tell which half. Even those who try to save everything will miss the really important, time and time again. Nevertheless, we try to beat the odds. Here then is a huge dilemma, because there are some spectacular instances demonstrating the importance of saving everything.

I have already mentioned the case of the Oxford dodo, saved from destruction at the last minute. In back-casting to try to recover the history of Aids, it turns out that over the past forty years, hospitals and laboratories had routinely saved hundreds of blood samples from both humans and non-human primates. These turned out to be essential in providing a possible time-line for the course of the disease. They allowed us, for example, to be sure that the disease was not spread by polio vaccines, as one theory propounded. Similarly, when Rachel Carson pointed out the dangers of DDT to nesting birds,[48] it was necessary to test the matter. Was it true that DDT caused a lethal weakness in the eggshells? How could one find out if eggshell thickness in ospreys was greater thirty years before or that it had changed in direct proportion to, and perfectly in time with, increased environmental levels of DDT? Easy, go to a museum. Some museums had thrown away their collections of eggshells. Some, including the Peabody Museum at Yale had not only saved them, they had saved the broken specimens – perfect for sampling and revealing the deadly correlation between use of DDT and eggshell thinning.[49]

It is almost impossible to produce a list of things that absolutely, unequivocally should *not* (in principle, at least) be collected and saved. People have collected used crack cocaine vials and the wheels of felted lint that collect in the filters of clothes dryers. Somewhere, perhaps, though God forbid, there is someone who collects old condoms and, worse, someone who finds serious scholarly value in them. (A friend who read this manuscript sent me a sample from his collection of unused condoms, an American GI issue of 1944!) Or a collection of dead house plants. At least one artist works with elephant excrement, and another has created, and is selling for charity, a limited edition of cow-dung casts.[50]

Given this never-never land where everything has worth, it is easy to see why museums never get rid of things, even though the economic facts of life dictate that they should. Which means that, unless they have been specifically constituted to resist growth, museums of every kind must inevitably grow and grow. However, there was nothing principled or pre-ordained about what we have already chosen to save and what we have not, and contemporary fashion is certainly no guide to long-term cultural worth and significance. Artists we haven't honoured might in fact have been worth the effort that nobody made – for example, women artists of the seventeenth and eighteenth centuries. Equally, of course, one suspects that many artists, especially modern artists, are being saved even though they don't command it. Damien Hirst, for example, may only be worth ten minutes of videotape fifty years from now; Jeff Koons slightly less. Perhaps one solution would be simply to keep a small number of 'samples'? Of course; but whom would you trust to make the right choices? It would not have been useful for the Aids research. Suppose that only three of the 2000 paintings left unsold after the death of Van Gogh had been kept – 'just to remember the crazy old boy by'?

And so – inevitably – there are collectors and there are museums, storing millions of objects for posterity. Microfilms and digitized three-dimensional colour pictures may help us deal with the volume problem, but then they also have to be created, processed and stored by someone, at someone else's expense. Because they may all become useful. But can it really be true that there is value in everything (assuming that information equates to value)? How much value? At what price? Are we forced, because we cannot foretell what will be important next, to treat everything as of equal cultural value? Must everything be saved?

All civilizations have measured their eternal worth in part by those material products of their arts and sciences that embody the values and beliefs of those societies. The question may be: Do all such products equally embody those values? In the last few centuries, and particularly in the last hundred and fifty years, we have worked to construct our own history in part by using not just the written documents but also all the 'objects' of history, in a sort of intellectual back-casting. We seem to have become obsessed with our history not just in order to avoid repeating it, but also to use it for our own ends – to justify and reify as well as to enlarge and improve our sense of ourselves. The truth is, we have become strangely dependent upon this back-casting for authentication of our roots, and (for some) for guilt-ridden apologies for our history. This deep need for cultural justification in material terms may be measured by the fact that someone recently told me in all seriousness that the transistor had been invented by his people in Central Africa in the 1850s. A long-standing symptom of all this has been our obsession with collecting and preserving everything we have done; hence the argument that everything has cultural value and must be saved, trash and all.

In the process, being good capitalists, we have seen that most of those cultural objects, so earnestly sought, can be translated into wealth. As that American institution of the tabloids, Ann Landers, is reported to have said: 'Anyone can become rich if he can guess exactly when a piece of junk becomes an antique.' Collecting older art, encouraging younger artists, looting ancient tombs, and even assembling and collecting utter junk have all constituted (as the old Tom Lehrer song put it) 'doing well by doing good'. Too bad Van Gogh didn't keep even more of his own work, and also his coffee cup, his belt, and underwear. We could have made a market for those. If he had saved his toenail clippings (didn't Picasso save his?), modern chemical analysis might tell us whether he was sick – although it could not tell us why he painted so wonderfully or, indeed, why his contemporaries thought his work was junk. And

then, of course, there is the ultimate Van Gogh collectable, his
razor – priceless.

The United States national anthem, like that of many nations, is
'difficult' and not just for its overly high notes:

> Oh say, can you see, by the dawn's early light,
> What so proudly we hailed in the twilight's last gleaming . . .

Foreigners wonder: What can they be talking about? It is, of
course, that 'our flag was still there'. Nothing could be more sym-
bolic to the American nation than that flag surviving the British
bombardment of Fort McHenry, Baltimore, in 1812. And it actually
is still there, as a tattered exhibit in the Smithsonian Institution.
Mr Bill Gates has recently offered to pay the bill of many millions
that will be needed to restore it ($18 million, to be precise). That's
wonderful – or is it? Is it merely a foolish sentimentality? The powerful symbolism of that flag exists independently of the object
itself. The flag that was still *there* is not required to be *here* and real,
or real and perfect again, any more than King Alfred's burnt cakes
or George Washington's cherry tree. Perhaps the flag's continuing
existence, especially renovated, in some way even diminishes it.
No one would argue that for the Magna Carta or the Declaration of
Independence, but is it necessary that every symbol be made
patent, every historical artefact saved? If not, who will choose?

While we can try to make money out of almost anything, we cannot reify everything in our culture. A great part, the most fundamental part, is intellectual. Objects are only a representation of
that foundation, a growth from it. (One can imagine other societies in which this material glorification of the past and present
would not merely be considered vulgar but intellectually empty,
an excuse for the real thing, a substitute for a real sense of history
and a real sense of who we are.) The most frustrating paradox of
all, perhaps, is that when we save something, preserve and cherish

it, we still do not quite have it. One could call this the 'bar-of-soap' problem – like the wet soap in the bath, the tighter we try to grab hold of it, the more likely it is to escape us. This is an essential part of the phenomenon of 'reconstructing reality'. The painting we own is not quite the same as the painting that left the artist's studio (especially if it is by someone like Mark Rothko, who was sometimes casual about the permanence of the paints he used). Ships like USS *Constitution* or HMS *Victory* are hardly original any more. As we save the ships, we restore them until perhaps less than 10 per cent of the wood is original. Some of it has been replaced more than once. And, of course, someone regrets the trees that were cut down to make the new planks. And so on. As Charles Frazier put it in his novel *Cold Mountain*:

> [There were] many songs that you could not say anybody in particular made by himself. A song went around from fiddler to fiddler and each one added something and took something away so that in time the song became a different thing from what it had been, barely recognizable in either tune or lyric. But you could not say the song had been improved, for as was true of all human effort, there was never advancement. Everything added meant something lost. And about as often as not the thing lost was preferable to the thing gained, so that over time we'd be lucky if we just broke even. [51]

Beyond all this, there is the fascinating situation that, without careful collecting followed by professional preservation, many objects would be lost to us that – like the Fort McHenry flag – were created to be entirely ephemeral. Many items that we covet and preserve, not just for their material beauty but also for their inherent meaning, were not meant to be saved at all. We would have little knowledge, for example, of early Australian aboriginal bark paintings if some had not been saved. Originally they were made on a new piece of bark with natural, water-based pigments. After the ceremonies for which they were made, they were discarded. It was important that they return to the earth. Aboriginals were offended, therefore, that their creations were interfered with by white strangers. Now creating bark painting is a major business and a not inconsiderable art. What has been lost? What has been gained?

With modern technology we can save many things even though collecting and preserving them changes their essence, their reality. Thus we might consider the famous fossil trackway at Laetoli in East Africa. Preserved in the fossilized mud of a lake shore are the footprints made by an adult and a child. But not just any footprints. Between two and three million years old, they are the oldest known evidence of our human ancestors walking erect. There is something infinitely touching – and literally a touching, a reaching out across the years – in the vision that these tracks conjure up, a mother walking with a child, the mother taking short steps and the child long ones to keep up. Once the tracks were exposed to the air and to scholars and visitors, they started to deteriorate. Infiltration of some kind of plastic resin into the delicate rock/mud may preserve them for ever, but not as they once were. Not as they were as fossils, and certainly not as they were on that day, millions of years ago, when a mother and child walked along the lake shore, hand in hand.

Must all the countless material objects, permanent or ephemeral, of our society be saved? Apparently our answer is 'yes' and to accomplish that goal we must apparently also transfer them from private to public ownership. But possibly our answer also implies that no one wants to take responsibility for deciding that something should not be saved.

As footnote, there is one final irony here – right in our own museums. Recently, some museums' displays have themselves come to be seen as entities that must also be saved. This is particularly the case in natural history museums and science museums, and grows naturally out of the fact that the public gets its experiences through the medium of particular exhibits. So, long after their scientific usefulness has expired, they become almost cultural landmarks. Some natural history dioramas have genuine artistic content, their background paintings being the work of artists like Knight, Jacques and Zallinger. But the especially bad ones have a kitsch quality that is equally compelling to a certain audience. The packaging and presentation have become collectable along with the content.

In the end, collecting is aimed both at the past and the future. The past, because we all need to understand, explain and justify our origins. The future, because in all our insecurity we need to guarantee that all our brilliance will be encapsulated for future generations to appreciate. So we try to save everything. In our passion for collecting everything, from the sublime to the utterly trivial, we have become like King Canute, only in reverse. Where he tried to prevent the tide from flowing in, we want desperately to prevent it from flowing out.

10

Three Museums: Three Stories

The ironic truth is that American companies are now performing so
badly precisely because they used to perform so well.

Michael Hammer and James Champy,

Re-engineering the Corporation, 1994

Very few people in the USA or Britain have heard of the Civic Center Museum in Philadelphia, yet it was once the leading museum of its kind in the whole world. Its story will remind us of the need for a driving mission for a museum or collection and the fact that we cannot automatically assume that all our museums will survive.

The 1893 Chicago World's Columbian Exposition brought to the United States the best that countries all over the world could offer in the way of material demonstrations of national identity and resources. What was to be done with all these objects when the exposition ended? A resourceful (in both senses) Philadelphia professor and business-man, the biologist William P. Wilson, bought them and had them shipped to Philadelphia. Over the years he added to his base the leftover materials from the then fashionable world's fairs (Paris, Budapest, Liberia, Guatemala, to say nothing of Nashville and Buffalo). By 1910 a great museum – the Philadelphia Commercial Museum – had arisen out of all these cast-offs, a highly functional one devoted to demonstration of the world's material goods, markets, and manufacturing prowess.

This truly was a commercial museum, a training resource and library for businessmen who wanted to venture into overseas markets and a visitors' guide to the American market-place. Nothing high-brow here, just good plain business information, including its own useful publications. It was all rather different from what we now think of as a museum, but in fact it was the very model of a museum in its strict functionality and its sense of mission and purpose, and the relevance of its collections. Then it died. In the 1920s, President Hoover's Federal Department of Commerce had taken over the museum's principal functions in foreign commerce. With Professor Wilson's death in 1927, its fate was sealed and the essential role of the Commercial Museum had shifted to Washington.

Eventually renamed the Civic Center Museum, the Philadelphia collections became a more usual, and distinctly more limited, sort of museum – essentially a display of curiosities from all over the world. Schoolchildren were here taught something of other world cultures, and reasonably successfully. As time passed, its collection of African artefacts (created a hundred years previously as tourist materials or trade goods) attracted the attention of scholars.[52] The museum could not survive financially, especially in competition with all the other institutions of the city and region. In 1962 the city council launched an ambitious plan for its revival as a showpiece for a city convention centre and new funds were raised,[53] but no one articulated what sort of a museum it could become. During the 1960s many of the collections were unaccountably destroyed and the more attractive of the remaining objects began to 'disappear' at an accelerating rate. In 1990 its doors were closed.

The museum still exists on paper, the remnants of its collections, ranging from dolls and African and Oceanic materials to a single brand-new Japanese motorcycle dating from 1953, are stored in a city warehouse watched over by a part-time curator. No one has had the courage to let go. Ironically, most of its archives are intact, and inevitably it has been proposed that *they* become the museum – a museum of a museum, as it were. Depending on your point of view this is either (for the archivist) an opportunity or (for the likes of Professor Wilson) the final insult.

Every region, in small towns and large, has its orphaned institutions like this, although perhaps not with so dramatic a history. Less obvious is the fact that many museums contain within them orphaned collections, no longer fashionable, where resources and interest have dwindled side by side. How many orphaned collections are there? How many will there be twenty years from now?

The Historical Society of Pennsylvania was founded in 1824 and serves as a massive archival resource, collecting and preserving historical, especially genealogical, records. In 1939 the society decided to branch out and to try to reach the public more widely on the basis of its large collections of historical artefacts. So the society became in part a museum. It was a logical, politically correct decision. But slowly the enlarged mission grew to be more than the organization could support. As funds dwindled, and with the earlier example of the collapse of the New York Historical Society in front of them, the board members decided in 1994 boldly to revert to the original mission to the exclusion of all else. This was a sound and sensible business decision but politically incorrect. The exhibition halls were closed, and a new library was planned to service the growing army of scholars using the archives. The society decided to de-accession its museum collections – the objects other than papers, books, and photographs – which it would now no longer use. A few very valuable objects would be sold to or exchanged with other museums – a painting of Governor and Mrs Thomas Mifflin by John Singleton Copley to the Philadelphia Museum of Art, for example. Failing an institutional home, the rest would go to auction. Such was the intention.

The society's collection of objects includes many trivia, such as a massive statue of the actor Edwin Forrest that seems to be there because it is too large to be stored anywhere else. More critical are items as diverse as two copies of the Declaration of Independence, the wampum belt given by the Lenape Indians to William Penn, a clock that belonged to Thomas Jefferson, a flintlock rifle taken from John Brown at Harper's Ferry, John Paul Jones' telescope, and so on. None of these would ever have heard the auctioneer's hammer but sale to institutions would have been quite logical. Exchange for other objects would have accomplished nothing, exchange for archival material would have been better. Outright gift would have been nice but the society needed something in return, preferably cash.

Once the plans for de-accessioning ('unloading', as the newspapers put it) the collections were announced, a howl of protest reverberated through the city. The argument was a familiar one: the society was being utterly derelict towards its duty and its 'public trust'. The collections of the society represented a public trust and must not be allowed to 'fall into private hands'. Little if anything was said about new funds. One of the plans that the society hoped would assist in their change of mission was a dream of a new, united Philadelphia historical museum that would take in a number of different regional historical collections and create one magnificent public museum. But who would pay for this? The president of the board of the small city-owned Atwater-Kent Museum stated rather endearingly: 'It's an important problem, a critical problem. The city and some of the motivated funders will have to solve it.'[54]

For the moment, the public outcry seems to have succeeded in causing the society to shelve its plans and to struggle on without the resources it desperately needs, caring for collections that it does not need.

The third story concerns The Academy of Natural Sciences of Philadelphia. It is useful to mention one of the larger American natural history museums because of the somewhat different dynamics and functions those institutions display. The United

States is home to many natural history museums of international scale and calibre in addition to the Smithsonian's National Museum of Natural History – including those in New York, Chicago, Pittsburgh, San Francisco and Cleveland. The oldest natural history museum in the country, the Academy of Natural Sciences, was founded in 1812 by seven men. These were amateur/professional scientists who were excited about the growth of American science, its increasing freedom from European influences, and the limitless opportunities in science presented by the western expansion of the United States.[55] The express purpose of the Academy of Natural Sciences was 'the acquisition and dissemination of useful knowledge' – a very Jeffersonian imprint. Soon, expeditions were sent all over North America and to many foreign countries. Huge collections were built up, the study of which revealed new wonders of the natural world – some of them even directly useful – in mineralogy, geology, anthropology, palaeontology, zoology, botany, and all their rarefied sub-disciplines.

As all this evolved, a fundamental change occurred. The original 'museum' had been nothing more than the pooled collections of the members, used to exemplify their studies and interests – specimens brought back as working samples for the future of science. The collection was the focus of the members' meetings, and any member could know all the collection. But as the collection grew, instead of being defined by and subservient to the aims of the academy – both practically and intellectually – the collections began to define the institution. Eventually, the scientific collections grew to the current level of approximately 25 million specimens, forming a resource of truly international significance. That being the case, almost none of the items is actually on exhibit, of course. Everything has changed. Having early opened its collections to the public, the institution soon became dual in purpose – a scholarly organization and a public one. As the years went by, the public museum changed from being a small array of sober, 'useful' exhibits aimed at a select group of members, to a series of displays focused on a general adult public. After the Second World War the focus shifted again to attract an audience of adults with children, while today the academy principally aims to attract children accompanied by adults. In its public exhibits, the academy early on adopted the only-too-familiar diet of 'dioramas and dinosaurs' – very much in the style of Charles Willson Peale's public museums (see page 18) and their successors rather than serious academies. In fact, for a long time now, the gate money of most natural history museums around the world has depended very heavily on the interest of children – mostly small (and getting younger) boys – in dinosaurs. What will happen when dinosaurs pall?

Sensibly, during the 1920s and 1930s the academy realized that it could not cover all of science from chemistry to anthropology. An exchange was made with the University of Pennsylvania, the academy acquiring botanical collections in return for which the Museum of Anthropology and Archeology took over care of the anthropology collections. Other collections were dispersed to what is now the Museum of the American Indian. Even so, the research enterprise is still necessarily spread rather thinly as it tries to cover natural history worldwide. On the other hand, however, attracted by the library and research collections, scientists from all over the world visit the academy to study. Relatively few of them are from Philadelphia, of course. And this is a crucial problem. This international institution, and many like it, is still essentially a private local one, supported in the Philadelphia area by local individual philanthropy, a shrinking corporate presence and a modest endowment. This presents something of a dilemma that is repeated in the large natural history museums of the United States. Who is to pay? Who in the immediate region has the breadth of interest and depth of pocket to subsidize the work of scholars of, say, Madagascan lizards or maintain huge collections of Andean birds and Asian snails? Biodiversity is a hot subject – funding it is somewhat more lukewarm.

I have highlighted the fates of just three museums in a single city. The lesson of these museums is that *mission* is crucial and must constantly be re-examined, and that there must always be a defined functional niche – a particular place and role – for each institution. It is not enough for the museum to be defined by its collections. Collections must be defined by a constantly evolving function. All too many museums stumble on, year after year, acquiring collections and responsibilities, without a thoroughgoing strategic review of their mission, the audience and their resources. Usually they harbour the forlorn – in fact, the doomed – hope that just a bit more money will solve all their problems. Not all collapse as dramatically as the Commercial Museum did. As T. S. Eliot reminded us, the end is usually a sad whimper.

11

The Paradox of Value
and the Dilemma of Ownership

What is a cynic? A man who knows the price of everything,
and the value of nothing.
Oscar Wilde, *Lady Windermere's Fan*, 1892

While we all tend to notice when some record price has been paid
at auction for a painting or manuscript, or there has been a major
theft, generally the public has no idea of the monetary value of the
collections in museums. Of all institutions likely to be accused of
Wilde's cynicism, museums trail in distant last place. They know
the intellectual worth of most things they own, but they typically
reject most notions of their monetary worth, even to the point of
not insuring most of their collections. Indeed, to insure so many
treasures would be cripplingly expensive. Only when *acquisition*
funds are inadequate (as they always are) or there is a spectacular
theft does the monetary value of the objects really enter into the
debate.

The paradox of value in museums is simply expressed. We have
concentrated a huge proportion of the world's greatest and most
valuable cultural treasures into institutions while at the same time
those institutions have significantly *not* thereby become any better off in terms of being able to pay for basic functions. It costs a
great deal of money to keep a successful museum going. The more
successful the museum in terms of its 'wealth', the greater the
required subsidy.

It is quite impossible to estimate the number of objects held in
the museums of the world, ranging as they do from broken arrow-
heads and dried bird skins to paintings, motor cars and frozen cul-

tures of DNA. It is doubly impossible to estimate their monetary value. In any other industry this would be not merely remiss, it would be incomprehensible. Indeed, the situation drives the accounting profession to distraction. How might one assign a value to these objects? Market price might work for some, but for most there is no market. Replacement value (i.e. the cost of digging in places near and far) would work for some material objects but not those of high creative content whose authors are, in any case, dead. The original cost adjusted for inflation could be another index, but that would not work for a flint spear head, a traditional weaving passed down over generations, or a painting by Van Gogh that never sold. The value claimed for tax purposes on the deed of gift? That simply begs the question. The earning potential of the objects in an exhibit? Yes, but, as we have seen, the bulk of collections, in large museums at least, are held for archival, comparative and scholarly purposes, not for public display.

However imperfectly one were to calculate, if there are some one to two billion items in the institutions of Britain and America (excluding books, manuscripts and archives), the total 'value' has to be in the tens or hundreds of billions (dollars or pounds, at this scale it scarcely matters). If we include books, manuscripts, letters and so on, the figure must be more than one trillion. Pretty soon, as Senator Dirkson once said of the US defence budget, we'll be talking about real money.

Basically, museums do not want to take on the considerable burden of trying to put a value on their collections. This is not because the objects are unique (any work of art) or too arcane (a collection of six rare moths from the Napa River in Ecuador), but because they have no intention of *using* those values, of testing them in the market-place, and do not want to be challenged to do so. Instead, institutions give all their objects a transcendental status, being philosophically opposed to the notion of valuing them in the same way as pork-belly futures or barrels of oil – because that value will never be realized. Once objects enter such collections they become, in this restricted sense, non-existent. Unfortunately, the museum's bills are not transcendental, but inconveniently material.

Institutions have been slow to realize (pardon the pun) the income-generating power of collections beyond putting on the huge blockbuster art shows upon which they have in part become dependent. The vast bulk of collections consists of lesser works sitting in the reference collections, not suitable for exhibit (especially as the public becomes more demandingly sophisticated). They are not generating income, but accumulating costs. What other kind of organization would tolerate that? The answer given is always that a 'public' institution has to operate on different rules. But how can it? The average art, history or science museum is not backed by someone with an open cheque book. Governmental museums, especially, have to balance their books and pay their bills like the rest of us. Equally, the public has also to be 'paid' in terms of access to the very collections it so poorly supports. Caesar has to be rendered unto!

All museums have a great deal they can 'sell' if only they can use their imaginations to create 'value added' products out of their vast holdings – images of art works, copies of old sound recordings, photographs, educational materials of every sort, all the miscellaneous matter on the shelves of the museum shop. Natural history museums have recently woken up to discover that they contain a resource of considerable value to the commercial and governmental sector. In their preserved specimens collected over a hundred years or more, and particularly in the data that is recorded with them – dates, places, names (the provenances) – is encoded the history of our changing environment. Or it would be if the data were better organized, electronically accessible, and analysed. From them we could trace the ebb and flow of natural populations, the spread of some species, the pushing out of others, the extinctions and introductions *and* the relationship of these to changes in agriculture, watersheds, climate – all this is potentially available in these collections. From abroad, where extinction is even more the rule, our museums have priceless collections of species that no one will ever see again. Nowadays one can extract DNA from these species and do wondrous things like trying (absurdly) to create a living mammoth (or, in the movies only, a dinosaur). With the wholesale destruction of natural environments, especially rainforests and grasslands, scientists in our museums are begged to go out and study – and collect – more. All of this represents potential income. Surely something parallel to this is encoded in the collections of other kinds of museums, especially if they pooled their data electronically.

While most institutions own large numbers of objects for which they receive no benefit in terms of a direct revenue stream, these objects may, paradoxically, be appreciating greatly in value. As the associated costs continue to rise, there is no equivalent of capital gains (fiscal or intellectual) or of dividend income. Therefore, the bigger the collection relative to the public functions, effectively the poorer the institution in purely fiscal terms – we are not talking here about moral or intellectual worth. This situation flows in part from yet another paradox, the paradox of ownership. Normally one would expect that any enterprise endowed with enormous resources would find a way to use those assets to finance the essential functions of the organization. That is what would happen in business. But museums are not businesses in that sense; paradoxically, they hold assets that they may not fully 'own'.

When the newspapers fulminate that some collection or other must never be allowed to fall into 'private hands' all sorts of questions are begged, misconceptions furthered, and mischief done. The public 'owns' the works in the British Museum and Washington's National Gallery of Art but not the Duke of Devonshire's Rembrandt or the Metropolitan Museum of Art's Vermeers. All the same, if the Duke or the Metropolitan should wish to sell their most famous paintings, the public 'interest', however confused its basis, would rapidly be felt. While private not-for-profit institutions are, in a sense, public institutions, when the public insists that an institution must care for objects 'held in public trust' the reality is that they are telling it to act like a private entity and to go out and look for some rich old ladies and generous corporations. When the time comes to write the cheques or vote the taxes, the public tends to be reticent – with marvellous exceptions such as the cities of St Louis and Denver in the USA, which have voted taxes specifically for the support of cultural institutions, and the growing largesse in Britain associated with the Lottery. This reticence is not just because they have different priorities (tending to be hung up on matters such as education, crime on the streets and healthcare), but in part also because they are hopelessly confused about who owns what and what it is all for.

We can add to this list of woes the matter of context. Museums, with their emphasis on collections of objects that necessarily pertain to the past, and less frequently to the present, naturally appear to stand for constancy rather than change. But the contexts in which museums find themselves change all the time. Even the great national or international museums have a changing audience, but the vast majority of museums are regional and their audiences change far more rapidly. The founding fathers of a particular museum had a definite notion of their mission and audience, but if the audience has changed so, surely, should the mission. The alternative is that the museum comes to be seen as some sort of cultural fossil working within some normative but increasingly irrelevant framework. This happens in every big town and city especially if the institution is located where a once affluent community has been replaced by office blocks and lower-income housing.

A particularly fascinating example of these shifts in context is provided by the Cartwright Hall Art Gallery in Bradford, founded at the height of Britain's dominance of the textile industry. Its collections are particularly strong in Old Masters and the Pre-Raphaelites. But Bradford is now home to Britain's largest concentration of people of Asian origin, and the Cartwright has responded by serving its new community with a fascinating array of acquisitions from modern Asian artists such as Jamini Roy and Anish Kapoor to contemporary works from other British and American artists. They have created a Gallery of Transcultural Arts and their magnificently illustrated new guidebook celebrates both the centenary of the city and the fiftieth year of independence for India and Pakistan. Here is a museum trying to move with the times and with its audiences in a most dramatic way as the new is merged with the old in every sense. Sadly, at the very moment I write this, Bradford is torn by racial violence; but one cannot help believe that bringing the cultures together in schools and museums is a better answer than trying to keep them apart.

Change comes through leadership. Day-to-day responsibility for most museums (especially in the United States) belongs with a board of trustees. These people are charged by the appropriate authority with the task of stewardship and provision is made in the charter of the institution for the fate of the assets of the museum should it fail (usually transfer to another not-for-profit organization). Technically, the trustees may own the building and its contents, including all the collections, and hire and fire the staff. Typically, trustees are not museum professionals. Instead they represent a cross-section of the wealthiest families and most influential corporations that the institution can attract. Many trustees agree to serve on boards in part because of the status it will bestow on them and the institution in turn hopes to attract trustees whose own status will boost the institution. Statisticians call this 'bootstrapping'. Trustees often have useful skills, or at least a strong interest in the subjects covered by the museum. They may simply be devoted public philanthropists. They may be, or may represent, members of the founding families or corporations (paradoxically, when this happens it may create a conflict of interest). The ideal trustee is strongly supportive in the three Ws – wealth, wisdom and work – but doesn't quite know enough to interfere with the activities of the staff. Interest in the workings of the institution is essential; interference is discouraged. By law they must have no financial interest in the institution and gain no other advantage (in the way of contracts for the corporations they represent, for example) from their service. It can be a time-consuming labour of love. On every board where I have served and on every board that has stood over me, there have been people of the finest character and deepest devotion to the interests of the institution. Every board has its real angels as well as those few who are looking for angles.[56]

Labour of love or not, here is an absurdity, because such a board of trustees has neither a professional status in this particular field nor any kind of real stake in the fiscal state of the operation. Unlike shareholders in a corporation, trustees neither gain nor suffer with the fortunes of the institution. They are responsible for a set of collections, the value of which might be as high as hundreds of millions, but they do not know what that figure actually is. They may know little of the scholarly fields that the institution supports. It is truly one of the last places (with universities) where one finds the best and the worst of old-time amateurism, the kind whose passing from the field of athletics many of us mourn. It would be much worse, of course, if museum boards were made up of micro-managing minor civil servants. The challenge is to find a governing structure that is independent of political fashions and at the same time truly responsible.

The typical museum is afforded a special status on the basis of serving a public charitable function. The traditional tests of this status are as follows. The institution should provide a service that government would otherwise have to provide; this service should be a significant public good; a considerable portion should be provided free of charge; and the trustees should receive no remuneration for their 'ownership' duties. Finally, there is an implicit expectation that salaries paid to the staff will be on the low side compared with comparable professionals in business. A museum normally meets these requirements fairly easily, especially the last, except that nowadays less and less may be provided free of charge. Obviously there are many grey areas here. Whereas the education of the public in matters of art, science, history or industry may be a function that the state might otherwise have to conduct itself, one could argue that the holding of large reserve or study collections does not fall into the category of immediate public interest. Most museums hold collections far removed from their immediate public missions. (Here again we see the conflict between local and global.) For example, there is probably no *essential* need in the education of the public in a Mid-West state or Cumbria that scholars in their museums should be experts in, say, the ants of small Micronesian islands, or the temple bells of a particular Himalayan village. (Obviously, I here exclude national museums and college and university museums whose research collections are part of a direct and broad educational mission.)

In the USA, museums receive full or partial remission of property taxes, and of taxes on earned and unearned revenues. Donors to charities such as museums are entitled to claim considerable tax relief with respect to donations of money or 'items in kind'. Museums usually pay taxes on gift shop sales but do not pay 'purchase' taxes on materials and services they buy in. (In Britain fewer such advantages apply to institutions, just as fewer tax advantages accrue to individuals who give money or objects to museums.) The scale of such indirect subsidy of museums in the USA is considerable. The forgone annual real estate taxes on a good-sized museum in an American city could easily exceed $2 million. An endowment of $50 million yields $1 million per year of income on which no tax is paid. In exchange for a $100,000 gift, a donor receives a federal tax break of some $73,000. It has been estimated that the subsidy by the US government via this route each year is $1.2 billion.[57] The effects are often more noticeable at the local level and many states are actively considering ways to reduce the impact of tax-exempt status. In these discussions, museums happily hide behind the skirts of their politically more powerful sister institutions: churches and universities.

In the last decade or so, however, as public funds have become in short supply and political philosophies have changed, governments at every level, on both sides of the Atlantic have tended to discover that their museums are surely independent institutions after all and really ought to pay more attention to 'earned income' and less to 'hand-outs'. Indeed, there seems to be a general trend towards weaning institutions away from public subsidy, or for regional government to expect funding from the centre. Libraries are a good example of this problem: everywhere regions are decreasing public library subsidies in order to transfer the burden to the 'private sector'. Applied across the board to museums, zoos, hospitals and universities as well, this could be considered a dereliction of public duty at best and a form of civic blackmail at worst. It is, however, exactly the sort of difficulty one would expect to encounter when the status and the function of institutions are unclear: are they public or private, are they necessary or a luxury? In difficult times (because of a genuine shortage of funds, or a shift of political philosophy), these institutions will suffer the worst of both worlds.

On the positive side, the management of most museums, if only because every penny counts for so much, tends to be very tight. Administrations are extremely efficient. Little money is wasted. Volunteer time is used to the maximum and without it, many museums would fail. However, the management of museums is rarely as flexible as the situation requires. Museums change direction and policy only very slowly and this may in considerable part be due to the fact that trustees, unlike shareholders, first seek consensus and compromise.

Perhaps the most gloriously positive aspect of museums is the level of quite unconditional philanthropy they engender even though the different tax regimes in Britain and the United States certainly affect the amount (and general climate) of such giving. The citizens of the United States, together with corporations and foundations, support their institutions financially at a level of generosity undreamed of in other countries. Corporations alone contributed some $150 billion to charitable purposes in 1997.[58] In Britain philanthropy largely proceeds independently of such tax advantages and should therefore be doubly appreciated.

Museums are also good for business. What had been dismissed as a myth turns out to be true: in the USA, cultural attractions in cities such as San Francisco and New York actually bring in more money than the sports teams. The same is surely true in London. The Cézanne show at the Philadelphia Museum of Art in 1996 was visited by 548,741 visitors, who brought an estimated $86.5 million in additional business to city hotels, shops and restaurants. *Renoir's Portraits*, the top museum box-office success in the world for 1997, drew 498,323 people to the Art Institute of Chicago at an average of more than 6000 per day.[59] The Royal Academy in London earned a net of some £5 million with its Monet exhibition in 1999. The Tate Modern drew over five million visitors in its first year of operation: that figure can be translated into more than £150 million in terms of income for transport, hotels, meals, shop sales, etc. This, plus a great deal of civic pride, is why cities and small towns all over the country have encouraged the development of new museums as a key to civic image, city centre redevelopment and economic success. But it is worth noting that despite these successes for their communities, the institutions just mentioned are still balanced on a fiscal knife-edge.

Many old industrial sites have in recent years been converted into museums, and in the process Britain has allowed the creation of some museums and science centres whose financial viability is doubtful and which have drawn visitors away from existing institutions rather than increasing the pool. A recent study suggests that, instead of delivering a healthy injection of new blood to the museum business, these new capital projects have merely added an extra burden of £29 million.[60]

Very few museums worldwide operate on a safely balanced budget. Many are in dire financial straits. To this situation we can add the incongruous fact that our national institutions – British Museum, Tate, Smithsonian, etc – are forced vigorously to compete with other institutions for private and corporate philanthropy. One constantly returns to the fact that our institutions own enormous assets but are essentially stymied: like the land-poor aristocrat, museums are collections-poor. They have insufficient resources to operate while their holdings are worth billions. They are essentially victims of their own historical successes. Their carefully acquired resources are not accessible, not transmutable. A critical question then becomes: why do museums not act more like businesses with respect to their assets? Why, for example, do museums not sell some of their collections? Why do museums not upgrade, cull or edit their collections as freely as did the collectors who brought them to the museums in the first place? Why do the collections weigh museums down instead of freeing them up?

The causes of this situation are complex. Very many collectors gave their works to museums with the legally binding condition that they would never be sold. Many older collections were even given with express requirements that they never even leave the building – the Smithsonian's Freer Collection being among the more prominent examples. Nowadays no self-respecting museum would accept gifts with such restrictions. Other collections or objects were purchased by public subscription or government funding. The immovability of these objects is understandable, as is that of another category to which some kind of moral protection against selling them pertains – the items of supreme national importance such as the pen Jefferson used to sign the Declaration of Independence or Van Dyke's portrait of Charles II. Equally, there may be a particular local association to be considered. Antony Gormley's 'Angel of the North' could never be moved from Gateshead to Bournemouth. A whole range of cultural objects clearly has important meaning that transcends the question of 'ownership'. The institution that happily owns these treasures owns part of a special cultural heritage, and definitely does so in public trust. This was a responsibility that the institution took on with the acquisition of the object (often quite unwittingly, of course) and now must consider a privilege.

A different logic applies, however, to the majority of an institution's collections. I would argue that, in general, a museum should have as much discretion and independence in the disposition of its collections as it had in their acquisition. The public trust with which the institution is endowed should carry with it equal parts of responsibility and independence – independence to make decisions and the authority to make changes. The acid test of this is that museums ought to be able to dispose of collections, if they can make the case. The codeword, the term that causes so much *angst* in museum circles, is 'de-accession'. De-accession could mean any mode of transfer of objects from a particular institution. We might as well be realistic, however, and acknowledge that it means 'sell'.

Most museums have collections that they can no longer afford to house and for which they have no immediate use. The obvious solution is to hand them over to another museum where they will remain as protected objects. This is dispersal, not de-accession in its gritty, full-blooded sense. And the problem is easy to see. If the National Maritime Museum in Greenwich, for example, were to disperse parts of its collections to six regional museums, there is a danger that the result will be that one huge and six small museums become one huge and six large museums. The equally obvious problem, of course, is that, as more and more museums run into resource problems and find they have collections they can no longer afford to house and have no immediate use for, there will be fewer museums capable of accepting such collections. Dispersal may only temporize.

Equally, if present museums are in difficulties, it would be folly except in rare cases to create more museums – better by far to place available resources into existing institutions. This means that the only long-term strategy to make any sense at all is one that limits and even reduces the size of present holdings, together with the formulation and implementation of nationwide strategies for justifying the funding of institutions and particularly for planning future collecting. Just how much 'museum' does each country or region want, and why, and how willing are we to pay for it?

In my opinion, museums should be encouraged, perhaps even required (if they are in receipt of public monies), constantly to jus- tify the size and nature of their collections and to maintain a strict business strategy for resource allocation and management. Per- haps not surprisingly, most strategic planning at present simply consists of looking for ways to continue things as they are. Howev- er, it does not seem unreasonable that museums should, wherever possible, upgrade their collections in a manner that increases qual- ity without increasing size. Choice and selectivity, not growth, should be the byword. Experience shows that de-accession can be a useful tool here; we should not reject it out of hand.

The philosophy of the principal professional associations in this regard has a strong flavour of political correctness. and complete unworldliness, and every appearance of an ostrich with its head in the sand (never mind that ostriches don't actually do that). The Museums Association of Great Britain, the American Association of Museums and the Association of Art Museum Directors, to whom the word 'de-accession' is about as popular as rain at an outdoor wedding, have tried to make it an article of faith that no collections should ever be de-accessioned.[61] And, on the rare occasions that they are, it is decreed, the proceeds of the sales must be used only to purchase more specimens. The *reductio ad absurdum* of this creed is that these new purchases must be made in the same areas as the originals. That is, one should not sell minerals to buy paintings, or insects to buy fossils. And one must never, never, *never* sell an object to create an endowment, to repair the roof, upgrade the air-conditioning or hire a technician.

Institutions fear that if de-accession were to occur regularly on a large scale, donations would be threatened. Logically, of course, this problem would disappear if all museums had the same policy. But resistance to de-accession is not based simply on practicalities or logic. It is based on the same utterly understandable, but maddeningly vague, principle of 'public trust' that promotes the aggressive annexation of cultural objects into quasi-public or fully public ownership in the first place and then takes away from the institution the flexibility of deciding that *this* item could go, but *that* must be retained. It precludes the institution, moreover, from making these decisions on any grounds at all – fiscal, professional, aesthetic or practical. At the same time, none of these theories and the systems they promote does anything to relieve the pressure on the museum – in fact, they act only to make things worse.[62] In other words, what counts as professional best practice contains the ultimate seeds of destruction of the very entity it is supposed to serve. No wonder, then, that there is a conflict between the fact that the institution 'owns' its objects and that it also 'holds them in public trust'. Any hard-pressed museum director has often asked the question: Which is it, for it cannot fully be both?

The institution owns the building, the computers, the storage cases. All are funded by the help of, or perhaps entirely by, the support of the public. The public that bought a computer for the museum registrar's office would not mind if the institution sold it. The public that may or may not have bought a particular painting insists that it can never be moved. As a matter of principle none must be sold. We have created a situation in which the collections are not *owned* in the same way as other assets. But we have not created agencies and strategies for dealing with the awesome responsibilities and inevitable consequences of this principle. Our only recourse is to beg for more money.

I would not argue that de-accession is the only answer, or even a major answer, to the problems of museums. But our inability to deal with the issue highlights the need for a strategic plan for the whole sector, a plan that does not assume the present undefined and potentially indefinite growth and at least considers the possibility that collections should strategically decrease in size.[63] I cannot in all conscience argue, either, that for some cultural objects to pass back into private hands is, as a matter of sacred principle, bad. Certainly libraries do not think so. Behind the appearance of purity, many institutions in fact do de-accession on a small, usually discreet, scale. Libraries seem to be attacked less for selling books at auction than museums are for selling works of art and it turns out that we are very selective – hypocritical, it might even seem – in our disapproval of de-accessions. For example, the Guggenheim Museum in New York sold three paintings (a Chagall, a Kandinsky and a Modigliani) for $47 million and, while there was a tremendous outcry, the result for the museum seems to have been wholly positive. Thomas Hoving, former director of the Metropolitan Museum of Art, has been artfully straightforward about that institution's wheelings and dealings.[64] There was no great outcry when, in a 1997 auction at Sotheby's, a number of decorative architectural items were sold by the Art Institute of Chicago, mostly from demolished English country and town houses. The case perfectly exemplifies museums' ambivalent position with respect to collections. It turns out that English period rooms are now unfashionable in major art museums. The Art Institute 'once had period rooms, but we got rid of them over 13 years ago when the museum was renovated.'[65] The fashion for such rooms did not last long: 'The period [1919–39] was the hey-day for demolition contractors, antique dealers, and decorators feeding American museums and collectors hungry for English interiors and furnishings.'[66] The reason for the change is one already noted: 'In today's world of cheap air travel, more Americans can go to Europe to see the real thing . . . the de-accessioning of period rooms is a trend that will continue.'[67] The result, furthermore, is perhaps a happy one. New owners are placing these furnishings – magnificent panelling and doorways – back into real houses (some back in England!) and the museum gets funds with which to do new things. It would be beyond stupidity if in this case the Art Institute were forced to buy more period room elements. It would have been wasteful for the pieces simply to sit unseen in storage where they would, arguably, be no safer.

This is hardly the place to review the complexities of the case law on ownership by not-for-profit institutions, as it not only differs between Britain and America but varies across the otherwise United States. However, it is worth noting that the subject often comes up in the related form of conflict over the use by universities of endowed funds. Just a few years ago a Connecticut court made the very sensible ruling (under the Uniform Management of Institutional Funds Act) that a donor to a college cannot sue the recipient in order to influence how a gift is used without compromising the tax write-off received at the time of the donation.[68] In other words, once a gift has been made, the receiver has discretion over how it will be used. One cannot give something away and still retain complete control over it. Amen to that! Such a principle should be strengthened to embolden museums to be more flexible with respect to de-accessions.

We could also benefit from more cases like the classic British court decision in Re Pinion (1965) affecting an artist who tried to give his collection to the National Trust. The court could conceive 'of no useful purpose' in 'foisting on the public this mass of junk'.[69]

Perhaps one can have too much of a good thing, but one rarely gets what one wants. In practice, we already have more museums than we can afford, larger collections than we can sensibly sustain, some collections that we do not need, very limited opportunities for creative growth in those sectors where growth will be expected, and even more limited opportunities for rationalization. The problem could be solved with the injection of more money, of course. But every segment of society needs more support. Museums – evidently – do not have the first call on the local, regional or national purse.

12

Changing the Culture

Who and where is the Forgotten Man . . . who will have to pay for it all?
William Graham Sumner, speech: 'The Forgotten Man', 1883

Laying up treasures on earth has become a major contemporary preoccupation, rivalled only perhaps by the parallel industry of creating those treasures on earth. The resulting cornucopia of art, nature and technology is more than just a passive emblem, a trophy, of our heritages. As the material embodiment of our cultures, our treasures encode our past and illuminate the present. How confidently we can use them to foresee the future, I do not know. In reality, however, our constructions of culture, past and present, are always based on incomplete evidence, the more so as we delve deeper into the past. In fact, our sense of our civilization has evolved in a strangely Darwinian way. Lacking a perfect record of the past, we have to build our cultural history out of fragments of the past, rather analogous to the chance mutations that nature throws in the path of evolving organisms. We take these scraps and make major landmarks out of them. They become the reality of our cultural past even though we cannot be sure that the true story might not have been somewhere else.

We and our predecessors have grown up not needing to know the exact authorship of Homer, the Bible or the Federalist Papers in order to value and use them. We have proceeded without knowing the works of the nameless men whose books perished with the fire at Alexandria in AD150. We know only a few poems by Catullus, and fewer than forty paintings by Vermeer survive, but we have virtually everything (good or bad) that Andy Warhol and Picasso ever produced. We desperately seek every further scrap of evidence of our material culture (and often, understandably, use them to bolster our existing views rather than produce new ones). There is both a powerful imperative to amass treasures on earth and a deep sense of frustration when we ponder what we might have lost. And equally a frustration when we wonder what we now ought to keep. Completeness, in every sense, then becomes the driving goal for our collecting and preserving. And it is equally understandable that the general will should be that as much as possible of these treasures should be in public rather than private ownership. Or at least there should be full public access.

Given the fragmentary nature of our cultural record, it is not surprising that we try to preserve everything. But can we afford it? Should we afford it? For England, I once formulated what I called the Next Four Miles Rule. As I drive friends from abroad around, showing them the beauty of the countryside and the charm of the villages and small towns, inevitably we come across a Georgian vicarage, an early Methodist chapel, a small country house with Elizabethan half-timbering, a Norman church, an Art Deco shop-front. Each building is in crisis – from dry rot, the aptly named death watch beetle, a falling roof, rising damp, the enthusiasms of previous restorations or modifications . . . Inevitably the friends exclaim at the urgency of saving such a lovely building: 'It only needs a few hundred thousand!' And then I point out that, as we continue driving, we will find another such structure begging for charity, each with its own 'thermometer' sign with the red of funds received still huddled at the base – and then we will find another, and another. Every four miles. The situation has greatly improved with the addition of Lottery funding and a general late 1990s affluence but the underlying problem remains: too many things – not enough money.

For some well-endowed museums, well-supported museums, museums that can flexibly move with their publics, for some tiny museums that are treasured by their communities, for large museums and great houses that are major attractions on the scale of Disneyland – for all these, there may be no fiscal problem. But the majority of institutions are run on shoe-string budgets compared with their responsibilities. Fundamentally, the problem mimics the principle articulated most famously by the Reverend Thomas Robert Malthus two hundred years ago. Referring to human populations and the economics of states, Malthus noted that populations grow geometrically but the food resources increase only arithmetically. The result is that populations must be kept in check either by dire agencies like war and pestilence, or by enlightened behaviour. Transferred to museums, we can restate the problem as follows: the needs of museums (existing museums and the constantly added new ones) grow geometrically while philanthropic and public resources grow arithmetically. The only solution is degradation of the state of the collections and reduction of services – or enlightened behaviour.

At certain periods of history, Malthus' predictions on population have seemed too severe and a poor model for human societies. At least three times in history, increased agricultural production (most recently through artificial fertilizers and genetic engineering) has dramatically reset the equation. Or perhaps merely reset the clock – progress here seems not to be indefinitely prolongable and populations have sky-rocketed. In museums, similarly, the blockbuster exhibition and the museum shop have created a whole new and significant source of income (and a non-trivial addition to the museum experience). In the last few years, exceptional stock market results increased the endowments of museums at a rate far exceeding inflation of operating costs. But again, the clock has merely been reset. The underlying resource problems remain.

And so we return to the 'owners'. In the world of government, what ministry or service has not planned furiously to manage the growth of health, education or defence? In the world of commerce, what board and shareholders would allow uncontrolled growth of the 'plant' without a parallel growth in true assets? What businesses would take on more and more assets over which they did not have full control or would allow other agencies to diminish that control? Who would develop products without a matching base of funded customers, or would even give free access to the product? What sensible business would place so much responsibility in trustees, many or most of whom have no businesslike responsibility to the organization, and who indeed are usually protected by various laws from the consequences of mismanagement? Why are the other 'owners', the public stakeholders, so far out of the loop? In the end, while the business of a museum is its objects, one of the objects of a museum is its business: museums form a real world in which a job has to be done, products have to be researched and tested, customers and markets found and serviced, assets increased, liabilities reduced, bills paid. But museums are not used to thinking in these terms. Too often museums have chosen simply to 'do good works' in the faith that, if the cause is good enough, support will appear – charity will always provide. I find this arrogant at worst and self-defeating at best. As a result of present trends, museums end up with more marketing staff and educators than conservators and curators, and more fundraisers than all of these. The public, who are asked to pay the bills both indirectly through taxes and directly through memberships and endless appeals for donations, deserve better.

Quite recently I sat at a meeting about a new organization where a noted television personality offered the opinion that a certain collection of books should only be accepted if it were 'as a working collection' because 'we don't want a museum'. The meaning was clear – that a museum was *not* a working institution but somehow merely a storehouse. On the contrary, museums and their collections should always serve big ideas. The idea of a museum used to be simple – elegant in concept and efficient in practice, as a small group of people made a direct connection between a set of objects and a driving vision of how to use them. Now there are as many visions as there are treasures. For some people it is the need to save for posterity an historical house or a ship. For others it is simply to own wonderful things. The vision might be deeply educational, or it might be mostly entertainment. The vision might depend on very few objects – even perhaps none at all (in the sense of permanent collections), others may require large comprehensive collections from the beginning. Some start as the vanity of a collector, some collections come to be seen and used by the public only after titanic struggles. Now we have a thousand different institutions and it is rather difficult to say what a museum is for, and for whom.

I hope I have not over-glamorized the museum business in Chapter Two. It is certainly a profession that many young people seek to enter, terrible salaries notwithstanding. Interestingly, however, in the last decade it has become increasingly difficult for major museums to recruit directors. Senior curators do not wish for promotion to a job that will take them away from the collections and scholarship, and reduce them to begging. There is little glamour in the hard slog to raise funds to keep an enterprise afloat. When asked what her daddy did for a living, one of my daughters once replied: 'He asks people for money.' Many boards of trustees have chosen their directors from among the so-called captains of industry, creating dual leadership: Mr/Ms Outside and Dr Inside.

After Malthus, Darwin naturally follows: 'We will now discuss in a little more detail the Struggle for Existence.' Soon every small town and college will have its own art gallery, historical and natural history museums, nature centre and science centre. Even more historic buildings will be placed in the public realm, more ships, trains and cars preserved. And more responsibility will be thrust upon the public to support them all. Very quickly there will be more museums in financial trouble. When museums start to fail – as indeed they are starting to do – pressure will be placed on the better funded ones to take over the orphans. Or, worse, collections will simply be left in warehouses, to face decay and oblivion. We face nothing less than Darwin's old Malthusian Grim Reaper. There is, at the moment, little if anything in the ways in which the museum world is internally structured or externally enabled to prevent it.

I have come to some very unpopular conclusions: that there are already too many museums; that it would be folly to create many more; that we have larger collections than we can sensibly maintain; that a lot of what we expensively hold in museums does not belong there; that we have very limited opportunities for innovation; and therefore that serious change is needed in order for the whole business to flourish.

Unfortunately, there are not many options for rescue. Of course one might hope that the subject will grow so important and large, or its problems loom so immensely, that governments will take over. If that is the right solution, then museums should profligately redouble their efforts to expand in every direction – and then call for help. Another strategy, also a huge risk, would be simply to do nothing, hang on by the fingernails, and see what happens. I suppose one could call that a strategy. It is what many institutions are now doing.

The answer probably lies in my grandmother's favourite maxim (usually produced at the most irritating times): The Lord helps those who help themselves. Subsidy without strategic planning rarely if ever produces healthy institutions. It is never a substitute for what must come first – a rigorously defined and ruthlessly pursued definition of purpose, assets and users. The only approach in every case must, I believe, be constantly to ask the single question: What makes a good museum? I believe that the answer does not lie in the size of the collections or even the greatness of the individual objects. It is not the breadth of coverage, nor the grandeur of the buildings, nor the merchandise in the gift shop, nor the food in the restaurant. A good museum is one that continually re-articulates its mission in relation to its stakeholders, its changing community needs, and its audiences of users and supporters. The successful museum then matches and adjusts its resources (even its collections) to that mission.

But more than that – far more than that – a dialogue is needed between the public and the whole museum community that will establish the ground rules within which each institution can create that strategic plan – a coherent social contract. Every aspect of such an institution has to be open to challenge and, potentially therefore, open to change. At the same time, if the nation wants a network of repositories for all the objects of material culture, it should fund that centrally.

Most of our great museums, having started with a single driving idea and purpose, have allowed their strengths to be diluted through growth and proliferation of efforts until they risk being overwhelmed. All too many have tried to serve an impossible number of public masters and public agendas. The library world is far ahead of the museum world in planning and consequently is far advanced in, for example, providing digital access to their holdings and, more to the point, persuading governments of the worth of what they do.

If resources are not to grow sufficiently (as almost by definition they will not) then museums must change. We must therefore constantly ask the difficult questions: Whose is this? What is it for? What is the product and who are the customers, now and in the future? Between collections and exhibits, which is the tail and which the dog? I have argued in this book that *mission* is crucial, and that a museum must be defined by its function rather than its collections. Collections that are not needed are not used and col-

lections that are not used are not needed. Collections left alone
soon decay. Money can help, but does not address the core problem.

Choice is hard, and one reason why museums avoid even the
exercise of identifying alternatives may be the fear that in the end
it might be hard to justify retaining some kinds of functions.
Choice might mean accepting broad restrictions on what one does
with public or private funding. Choice might mean allowing large
numbers of objects to pass back to or remain in private hands.
Choice might mean refusing to take on a responsibility for certain
classes of 'heritage' objects. Choice will mean allowing museums
to fail. Choice will almost certainly mean rationalization of collections to create centres of excellence, and focused rather than
catholic acquisition policies. Choice certainly means refusing any
object that is not accompanied by the financial resources to support it. In the future museums will no longer be defined by their
collections but collections will be defined by museums.

To many museum people these kinds of choices are like asking
the condemned man to choose between the noose and a bullet.
None the less, the more I write and talk about the future of museums, the more I hear about groups getting together to try to think
about a different, leaner, more strategically planned future. And
so, in the end, my optimism for the world of treasures on earth
and my joy at working in museums are undiminished. Bruised
and battered, perhaps, after a long time of trying to fund museums through some secular version of the miracle of the loaves
and fishes, but undiminished.

Notes

1 The exact number of museums and/or collections in the United States
(not held by individuals) is almost impossible to determine. Part of the
problem is that it is difficult to define exactly what a museum or collection is. Should one count zoos, arboreta, local historical association
collections and so on? Should one count institutions with no paid
staff?

Not all museums claim tax relief from the Internal Revenue Service
under the rubric of 501(c)3 status, or comparable status in the laws of
the United States; some museums are run as for-profit organizations or
as part of for-profit organizations; others exist as part of larger non-
profit-making enterprises (university collections, for example).

The American Association of Museums, based in Washington DC,
has some 2900 member institutions and estimates that there are 8500
museums all told. The Association's *Official Museum Directory, 1998*
(National Register Publishing Company, New Providence, NJ) lists
some 7700 institutions, but many museums and collections are not
listed there, especially the small ones. For example, for the Common-
wealth of Pennsylvania the *Directory* lists 356 institutions, whereas a
Commonwealth-compiled list numbers approximately 1000 museums
and collections. If this pattern holds true for the whole country,
15,000–20,000 may be a conservative number for the total number of
museums and collections in the USA.

2 V. Middleton, *New Visions for Museums in the 21st Century*, London:
Association of Independent Museums, 2001. For a discussion of the rate
of founding of museums in the United States, see Stephen Weil,
Rethinking the Museum, Smithsonian Institution Press, 1990 (especially
Chapter One: 'Enough Museums?'). Weil points out that half the muse-
ums in the USA were founded after 1950.

3 A. Babbidge, 'UK Museums: Safe and Sound?', *Cultural Trends*, 37, 2001.
Middleton, op. cit.

4 Most of the notes appended to this book do not come from what we,
the museum professionals, say about ourselves in professional books
and journals, but from what the press reports about us.

5 Charles Waterton's most famous book is *Wanderings in South America*
(1825).

6 *The Art of Collecting: Thirty Years in Retrospect*: Kimbell Art Museum, Fort Worth, 1995.

7 K. S. Thomson, *HMS Beagle: The Story of Darwin's Ship*, New York: W. W. Norton, 1995.

8 W. S. W. Ruschenberger, *A Notice on the Origin, Progress, and Present Constitution of the Academy of Natural Sciences of Philadelphia*, Philadelphia: Collins, 1852. See also: Toby A. Appel, 'Science, popular culture and profit: Peale's Philadelphia Museum', *Journal of the Society of Bibliography of Natural History*, 9: 619–34., 1980; Charles C. Sellers, *Mr Peale's Museum*, New York: W. W. Norton, 1979.

9 See Peale's great painting: *The Exhumation of the Mastodon*, Hessiches Landesmuseum, Darmstadt.

10 Albert C. Barnes, *The Art in Painting*, Merion, Pennsylvania: Barnes Foundation, 1925.

11 Name withheld to protect the guilty.

12 Exhibition: *Rodin and Michelangelo: A Study in Artistic Inspiration*, organized by the Philadelphia Museum of Art and the Casa Buonarroti, Florence, 1997.

13 Exhibition: *Bonnard, Rothko: Color and Light*, New York: Wildenstein, Pace Wildenstein, 1997.

14 Donna Haraway, *Primate Visions: Race and Nature in the Work of Modern Science*, New York: Routledge, 1989.

15 Richard B. Freeman, *British Natural History Books, 1495–1900: A Handlist*, Folkestone: Dawson and Sons, 1980.

16 Richard B. Freeman, *The Works of Charles Darwin, an annotated bibliographical handlist*, 2nd edn, revised and enlarged, Folkestone: W. Dawson and Sons, 1977.

17 Lynn H. Nicholas, *The Rape of Europa: The Fate of Europe's Treasures in the Third Reich and the Second World War*, New York: Knopf, 1994. Hector Feliciano, *The Lost Museum: The Nazi Conspiracy to Steal the World's Greatest Art*, revised edn, New York: Basic Books, 1997.

18 A Texan named Joe Tom Meador is stated to have stolen the magnificent set of works known as the Quedlinburg Treasure – twelve medieval church relics that had been hidden in a cave towards the end of the war as invasion by the Allies seemed inevitable. After Meador's death, his brother and sister were left with the problem of what to do with the works. Instead of doing the honourable thing and turning them in, they apparently sold the objects in Europe for $2.75 million (probably a fraction of their real worth). At this point the whereabouts and history of the Treasure became public. A federal case against the family and their lawyer fell on a technicality and, according to a report in the *New York*

Times (14 April 1998) it is unlikely that a prosecution will now succeed. The government may have the last laugh, however (not that laughter is appropriate in this sorry affair): the family may owe back taxes of some $50 million!

19 'Chinks found in museum's armor', *Philadelphia Inquirer*, 25 January 1998. Of course, a museum that has purchased a work that turns out to be tainted may often be stuck with a serious financial loss. An interesting device that may encourage museums to repatriate objects has been tested by the Wadsworth Atheneum, Hartford, Connecticut. In exchange for returning a painting that the Wadsworth purchased in good faith many years ago, the museum will get an important Caravaggio show from Italy.

20 For at least thirty years, federal and state laws have granted a sort of immunity against such claims for travelling art objects. The New York District Attorney argued that the works in this case were evidence of a crime and thus that protection did not apply.

21 Jonathan Petropoulos, *Art as Politics in the Third Reich*, Chapel Hill: University of North Carolina, 1966.

22 Hilliard T. Goldfarb, *The Isabella Stewart Gardner Museum*, Yale University Press, 1995.

23 'Boston art caper (cont.): The art of the deal', *New York Times*, 13 January 1998.

24 Early in 1998, fourteen works by the American primitive painter Grandma Moses were anonymously returned to the Bennington Museum. They had been bequeathed to the museum several years earlier but were stolen before they could be handed over.

25 Barbara Strachey and Jayne Samuels, *Mary Berenson: A Self-Portrait from her Letters and Diaries*, London: Victor Gollancz, 1983.

26 Strachey and Samuels, op. cit. p. 85.

27 *Masterpieces of Impressionism and Post-Impressionism: The Annenberg Collection*, National Gallery of Art, Washington DC, 1990.

28 Edward J. Sozanski, 'The Annenberg stars: what the Annenberg collections says about its collector', *Philadelphia Inquirer*, 28 May 1989.

29 The collection, along with its sister collection at the Walker Art Gallery, Baltimore, was displayed at the Royal Academy in London during the summer of 2001. See also *Gallery Guide: The Cone Collection*, Baltimore Museum of Art, 1989.

30 George H. Marcus (ed.), *Encounters with Modern Art: The Reminiscences of Nannette F. Rothschild*, Philadelphia Museum of Art, 1997.

31 Harvey S. Miller, quoted in *Philadelphia Inquirer*, 9 March 1997.

32 See *Great French Paintings from the Barnes Collection*, New York:

Knopf, and Lincoln University Press, 1993.

33 Howard Greenfeld, *The Devil and Dr Barnes*, New York: Viking Press, 1967.

34 The medical leech museum is in Charleston, South Carolina; the Spam Museum will be in Austin, Minnesota; the Boothroyd Museum is planned for Sandwell, West Bromwich.

35 For example, in 1997, Christie's in New York, under pressure, withdrew from auction a collection of nineteenth-century slavery documents.

36 'The public's trust', *Philadelphia Inquirer*, 10 August 1997.

37 Tony Hillerman, *Talking God*, London: HarperCollins, 1989.

38 Babbidge, op. cit.

39 *A New Vision for England's Museums*, London: Resource, 2001.

40 J. E. Grey, 'On Museums, their use and improvement', *Annals and Magazines of Natural History*, 1864, quoted by Mary P. Winsor, *Reading the Shape of Nature*, University of Chicago Press, 1991.

41 See, for example, Tom N. Tumbusch (ed.), *Tomart's Price Guide to Radio Premiums and Cereal Box Collectibles*, Chilton Publications, 1991.

42 'McCollectors', *Philadelphia Inquirer*, 31 July 1997.

43 'History society history', *Philadelphia Inquirer*, 28 July 1997.

44 See, for example, *Erica Rand, Barbie's Queer Accessories*, Durham, North Carolina: Duke University Press, 1997.

45 And the prices as well. Among the dozen or so books dealing with the prices of Barbie dolls and paraphernalia is Sibyl DeWein and Joan Ashabramer, *The Collector's Encyclopedia of Barbie Dolls and Collectibles*, Paducah, Kentucky: Collector Books, 1977.

46 Possibly every kind of toy already is being saved and collected. Surely Sharon Korbeck (ed.), *Toys and Prices*, Iola, Wisconsin: Krause Publications, 1998, which lists prices for some 18,000 different kinds, represents only a small drop in a very large bucket.

47 'McCollectors', *Philadelphia Inquirer*, op. cit.

48 Rachel Carson, *Silent Spring*, Boston: Houghton Mifflin, 1962.

49 Summary in F. Cooke, 'Pesticides and eggshell formation', *Symposia of the Zoological Society of London*, 35: 339–61, 1975.

50 Louise Neri, *Les Infos du Paradis*: 'Not Vital, Common Currency', *Parkett*, volume 33: 144–6, 1992.

51 Charles Frazier, *Cold Mountain*, Atlantic Monthly Press, 1997.

52 Harold D. Gunn, *A Handbook of the African Collections of the Commercial Museum*, Philadelphia, no publisher, n.d.

53 Ruth H. Hunter, *The Trade and Convention Center of Philadelphia: Its Birth and Renascence*, City of Philadelphia, 1963.

54 Fred H. Linquist, quoted in 'A move to join museum forces', *Philadelphia Inquirer*, 3 August 1997.

55 Patricia Tyson Stroud, 'The founding of the Academy of Natural Sciences of Philadelphia in 1812 and its Journal in 1817', *Archives of Natural History*, 22: 221–33, 1995.

56 Happily not everyone espouses the cynical views of one Albert J. Dunlap: 'Corporate charity exists so the CEOs can collect awards, plaques and honors, so they can sit on a dais and be adored.' *Mean Business*, New York: Simon and Schuster, 1996.

57 'Generous to a fault', *New York Times*, 2 July 1997; correction, 3 July 1997. See also note 44.

58 'Corporations oppose idea of telling how they contribute to charities', *New York Times*, 3 April 1998. Again, see note 44.

59 *The Art Newspaper*, International Edition, February 1998.

60 Babbidge, op. cit.

61 American Association of Museums, Code of Conduct, 1995. See discussion by Patricia Failing, 'De-accessioning: a sorry drama', *ARTnews*, September 1997. Draft Code of Ethics, Museums Association, 2001.

62 Glen D. Lowry, 'Taking the Lid off the Cookie Jar', *ARTnews*, March 1998.

63 See note 39.

64 Thomas Hoving, *Making the Mummies Dance: Inside the Metropolitan Museum of Art*, New York: Simon and Schuster, 1993.

65 Eileen Harakal, Art Institute of Chicago, interviewed by the *New York Times*, 20 October 1997.

66 John Harris, 'Moving Rooms: a History of the Period Room', in *English Furniture and Decorations*, New York: Sotheby's, auction catalogue (sale 7029), 1997.

67 John Harris, interviewed by the *New York Times*, 20 October 1997.

68 'Court says college donors cannot sue over gifts', *New York Times*, 18 August 1997.

69 *Tudor on Charities*, 8th edn, 1995, p. 50.

Index